I0787992

SLAY YOUR LEGACY:

9 KEYS TO MANIFESTING THE LIFE YOU WANT

SLAY YOUR LEGACY: 9 KEYS TO MANIFESTING THE LIFE YOU WANT
COMPILED BY: Charron Monaye

© 2020

ALL RIGHTS RESERVED. No part of this book may be reproduced in any written, electronic, recording, or photocopying without written permission of the publisher or author. The exception would be in the case of brief quotations embodied in the critical articles or reviews and pages where permission is specifically granted by the publisher or author.

PUBLISHED BY: Pen Legacy® (penlegacy.com)
TYPESETTING & LAYOUT BY: Junnita Jackson
(theliarscraft.com)
COVER DESIGN BY: Christian Cuan
EDITING BY: Carla Dean

DISCLAIMER

Although you may find the teachings, life lessons and examples in this book to be useful, the book is sold with the understanding that neither the co-authors nor Pen Legacy, LLC. are engaged in presenting any legal, relationship, financial, emotional, or health advice.

Library of Congress Cataloging – in- Publication Data has been applied for.

ISBN: 978-1-7333964-7-9

PRINTED IN THE UNITED STATES OF AMERICA.

Table of Contents

Who Is The Woman Behind The Brand, Pen Legacy??

Ever since she was a second-grade student in Ms. Jones' classroom at Prince Hall Elementary School in Philadelphia, Charron's journey as a writer was ordained. As a youngster, Charron would express herself through her gift of gab during class – questioning everything and debating her ideas. "Charron is going to be a great writer one day because she talks too much," Ms. Jones once shared with Charron's mother. Even though Charron's mother didn't approve of her daughter's excessive talking, she would later learn that Ms. Jones' thoughts were right and would pay off for Charron.

In 1993, Charron's poem "Alone" won a poetry contest. In that same year, she became an author when she published her book titled Tears on Fire. From that moment, Charron continued to hone her skills as a poet and submit her works to various poetry outlets, which landed her publishing opportunities and collaboration placements. However, it wasn't until accepted as a Staff Writer for the Philadelphia Association of Paralegals that she started to believe she "had a way with words". Her writing journey as a paralegal/law educator led her to interview celebrities, politicians, and cover events for CNN IReport. From First Lady Obama to Maya Angelou's funeral, Charron was the go-to person successful in penning articles that people wanted to read. Then came growth.

In 2008, Charron came up with the name Pen Legacy, which would become the publishing house within BMI and house her songwriting catalog that included song titles "Better Days", "I Apologize", "Lonely Days", "Commitment", and many more. This endeavor gave Charron leverage in the writing world and access to the greats in music. It even resulted in her being an attendee at many of the Recording Academy (Grammy Awards) event. Back then, she went by the pseudonym Soulful Michelle because she wrote soulful stories of love, pain, and desire.

In 2010, Charron changed her pseudonym to Charron Monaye and released her first solo book on November 4th under Purposeful Publishing titled My Side of the Story. Then, in 2011, she converted her first book and expanded the scope of Pen Legacy to include her theatre & film production team with her first theatre play, Living Your Life, birthed along with Pink Star Entertainment. She went on to release another book under Purposeful Publishing in 2012 titled Living, Loving, Laughing My Way Through. Shortly after that, Summer Fitch, Charron's sorority sister, encouraged Charron to start her own publishing company to help those who are looking to embark on the journey of authorship. With Charron possessing love, knowledge, and passion for writing, Summer knew it would be guaranteed that Charron would assist clients with patience and provide quality work. In 2015, taking the advice of her sorority sister, Charron added on to the legacy what would soon be her greatest entity, Pen Legacy Publishing. This lane would include not only her previous published books through Purposeful Publishing, but it would afford her the platform to extend her knowledge and expertise to those who were interested in learning how to become a published author. Then, in 2017, Charron had the honor of studying under American producer, television and film writer, and author Shonda Rhimes when she took Shonda's "Writing for Television" course. While in the course, Charron became proficient in writing and editing scripts, pitching scripts, creating memorable characters, writing story bibles, etc.

With eleven years of operating Pen Legacy®, five years of book publishing, twenty-six years of being a writer and published author, and still surviving in three industries – music, theatre, and literary – what more can you say! Pen Legacy is Charron Monaye. She is the legacy she is creating for everyone else. Congratulations to Charron, a woman who didn't let any grass grow under her feet and was willing to invest and elevate to stay relevant to the needs of her listeners, theatergoers, and readers.

What Does It Mean to Slay Your Legacy?

By: Andrel Harris

Positive or not, your past shapes your belief system, and what you've learned through your experiences molds your future. Therefore, you owe it to yourself to live up to your full potential, tackle your self-limiting beliefs, and operate in your purpose.

Going through various phases of your life will yield many lessons, each of which will make you stronger or deter you from your destined path. It is not what happens to you that separates the winners from the losers on this path; it's about how you triumph over the challenges.

Being an entrepreneur is no exception. In addition to the lessons you will learn along the way, you'll also have to make some sacrifices. No matter what aspirations you have, there is one thing for sure; there's a price you have to pay to get what you want. I've heard this saying in the beginning stages of my entrepreneurial journey but had no idea what that meant. An older gentleman, who was the head of a real estate club, was sending out emails for people to join a mastermind group. I recall receiving the invitation and reading the expectations, followed by the closing question, "Are you willing to pay the price to be successful?" In my response, I posed the question, "How much does this cost?" assuming he was seeking monetary compensation. He replied, "Are you willing to do what it takes to be successful? There's no cost to join." Believe it or not, it took a few years after that for me to grasp the concept.

You see, you have to be willing to do what others won't. To obtain something, you have to be willing to give up something to get something in return. You may have to give up your time, money, or energy. One of the most profound sacrifices you may need to make is changing who you are for the person you want to become. For many years, I had the mindset of trying to prove to everyone that my life was all together, mainly my finances. From the outside looking in, it appeared that way, but in actuality, I was deep in debt and living paycheck to paycheck due to the recession. What was interesting about meeting with the group was that when I arrived, I was the only flashy one. My car was newer, my house newly built, and my clothing was name brand. Yet, I was trying to pull myself together behind closed doors. I noticed that everyone else (who were all Caucasian) was in a better financial position than me. I recall the older gentleman asking me out of frustration with our team results, "How many pairs of feet do you have?" He asked this question because he knew I loved shoes, often wearing a different pair for every meeting. Yet, I was struggling to hit our emergency fund goal of $10k.

It took a while, but I finally understood what he was saying and realized I had to shift my thinking. I had to focus on having the desired life that I wanted versus appearing to have the life I wanted. I no longer cared what people thought, and I took drastic measures to pull myself out of financial distress. I even went as far as to do a 365-Day No-Spend challenge that went viral and ended up with a feature in Forbes Magazine. I was serious about changing the trajectory of my future.

When sacrificing who you are, you'll have to shift the habits you indulge in and maybe your values, as well. Be willing to give up the old you, which will require you to upgrade your relationships. You can't grow if you're the smartest person in the group, and your current circle may not understand your mindset and visions. Since your network is a significant component of your success, it would benefit you to surround yourself with likeminded individuals.

Speaking of network, I met Charron virtually through a book collaboration project. As a result of this connection, my manifestations are coming to fruition faster because I now network with winners. For instance, I had a vision of being displayed in Times Square but had no idea how I was going to make that happen. I soon realized Charron had the connection. Now take a moment to soak in how powerful it is when aligning with the right people. Not only that, but Charron and I are practically business twins. Working a full-time job and being an entrepreneur requires a certain level of tenacity. When I saw Charron's dedication to managing her business, I had no idea she worked another job full-time, too. She thought the same of me. Entrepreneurs may make it look easy, but believe me when I tell you, building brands to leave a legacy requires hard work and dedication.

If you are committed to keeping God first, making the necessary adjustments, and believing in your ability to make things happen, there's a great reward that awaits you. You will birth your legacy. Lastly, I need you to confront yourself and don't allow you to hold you back. Leaving a legacy is an essential part of your life's purpose. Someone is depending on your contributions to the world. One for sure way to contribute to others is by becoming an author. Since every one of us has a story inside of us, you can share your message, and in turn, it may help others. Also, books serve as passive income. Therefore, not only are you helping others, but you will be helping yourself, as well. Pause and think about this for a second; failing to commit to bettering yourself will result in unfulfilled dreams and missing out on what you want most out of life. You owe it to yourself to Slay Your Legacy.

Back Down Memory Lane With Pen Legacy

Charron Monaye
Author, Poet, Lyricist
Are you ready to
hear my side of
the story?
WWW.CHARRONMONAYE.COM

TINESHA BOSWELL
DON'T
GIVE U
TOO SOO
CHARRON
MONAH
ove

Meet The Pen Legacy Team

Founder: Charron Monaye
Co-Founder: Christopher Hopson
Administrative Assistant: Karen Langley
Editor: Carla Dean
Web Designer: Christian Cuan
Graphic Designer(s): Junnita Jackson & Christian Cuan
Typesetter: Junnita Jackson & Carla Dean
Public Relations: Madison Jaye
Attorney: Toni Moore, Esq
Accountant: KMB Tax Services

The 9 Keys of Our Legacy

Kiawana Leaf

Life can be brutal, unforgiving, and beautiful all at the same time. For Kiawana "Key" Leaf, she's experienced this and a whole lot more. A self-made entrepreneur, author, actress, and inspirational speaker, Kiawana aspires to inspire, empower, and embrace millennials across the nation. To heal from traumatic events in their life, find, and fulfill their purpose and women who are survivors of domestic abuse through her first business venture, Empower Too Inspire, LLC. The foundation of Empower Too Inspire is built on Women's Empowerment and Kingdom Advancement.

Kiawana is a rising star who was featured on TV One's "For My Man" and Ari Squires' soul stirring documentary "No More Chains 2". While life has thrown many obstacles her way, Kiawana's faith in God has never wavered. She dedicated her life to Jesus Christ at the age of twelve. Kiawana's greatest inspiration comes from her greatest joy–her daughter, Azariah. Kiawana looks forward to being an inspiration to many who are seeking healing and spiritual growth. It is her dream, vision, purpose, and power to Empower Too Inspire!

Contact Info:
Business Website: www.empowertooinspire.org
Author Website: www.kiawanaleaf.com
Business/Author Email:
Kiawanaleaf@empowertooinspire.org
Facebook: Kiawana Leaf
Instagram: @Kiawana___ & @Empowertooinspire

They Ask Me How I Made It!

"Faith," I respond. Jokingly, they brush me off and dismiss my answer. Repeatedly, I am asked by multiple people, "Key, how did you make it?" My response is always the same. It never changes. "Faith," I reply once again, but faith without works is dead. As I embarked on my journey as an author, elevation was my only option. I was a 25-year-old single mother who felt stuck on a job. Because of demolished credit, I was struggling with my finances and barely making ends meet. Somewhere along the way I lost my voice, identity, faith, and strength. Not only was I battling my insecurities, but I was also grieving the loss of my childhood best friend. I literally felt my life turn upside down and found myself living in a dark, shallow place.

In darkness, people usually crave light, but as crazy as it may seem, I was content. I was painfully comfortable in my dark, shallow place. Sure, I desired a *"healthy peace"* and a change for the better! However, I didn't really want to work for it. I was settled at my job, enjoying the favors, leisure, and lack of intense work. With all of life's calamities smacking me in the face at once, peace seemed impossible for me to find, especially since I wasn't actively seeking it. In my head, I made the assumption that this elusive peace would just come! In retrospect, I understand that was a crazy expectation, but I was not alone in my erroneous thinking. Many people sincerely believe that things are supposed to just happen. I couldn't seem to catch a break and always told myself and God that something had to change. Have you ever experienced that lost feeling in the middle of a storm, test, trial, or tribulation? Have you felt stuck, unable to find an escape while bombarded with one thing after another?

I recall sitting in the middle of my bedroom floor and crying out to God, *"Why? What is it going to take? Why am I going through this? What is your purpose for my life?"* Little did I know, He was birthing greatness in me for His glory. It is easy to look at life's calamities and focus on the negative. It has been said that only the strong survive. In the midst of my storm, I most definitely didn't believe I was strong enough.

I picked up a pen and began putting all my feelings and thoughts on paper. I imagined that I was sitting with a therapist, completely releasing everything bottled up inside of me. As therapeutic, relaxing, inspiring, and encouraging I knew my story would be, it did not alter the fact that I disliked writing. Furthermore, fear gripped me. I was afraid to admit and share the most uncomfortable and traumatic events of my life. Embracing my vulnerability and being completely transparent would allow everyone to see the real Key. The thought of that exposure was embarrassing to me.

I scratched the surface of entrepreneurship in 2017 when I launched "InspiHer". Not being proficient, dedicated, or committed to my new business, I ran into many obstacles and setbacks. Becoming discouraged and overwhelmed, I abandoned the venture. My timid demeanor was a hindrance. I lacked the self-confidence and faith necessary to complete tasks successfully. Although I gave up on "InspiHer", God did not give up on who He destined me to be. I received the prophecy that God called me to be an entrepreneur in January 2018. As I reflected on the prophecy, I questioned God. *Entrepreneur of what?* I was not comfortable with my responsibilities after launching "InspiHer". I had already unsuccessfully attempted entrepreneurship. What exactly was God's assignment for me?

Through my personal, mental, emotional, and spiritual growth, I began developing a hunger to use my voice to share my story. I was desperate to be a vessel of grace. I knew God didn't allow me to overcome and survive turbulent times just for me. I was afraid. I feared I was not qualified, and I did not look like a stereotypical church member. So many excuses filled my head. I was running from who God had called me to be. As bad as I wanted to use my voice to share my story, I didn't know how to proceed. I wasn't confident standing in front of others. I worried others would judge me and that I would not be accepted. Although I feared no one would support me, I desired to live my purpose!

I knew this feeling was God pushing me to move as I grew deeper and stronger in Christ. No longer able to ignore my assignment, it became a burning desire in my belly that had to be birthed! When I stopped pretending, I had not received the entrepreneurship prophecy, I started hearing from God. I began deeply evaluating myself, removing people and things that were hindering my healing and growth, instituting a lifestyle of fasting, praying, and attending church.

These simple lifestyle changes were life-altering. It may not seem like much, but it's not as easy as it sounds. It was a major adjustment and a sacrifice to leave my comfort zone. I didn't party and drink as I did before. Everything had to change – my environment, my attitude, and my affiliations. It was necessary to connect with people who fit my future and to properly budget my finances. I also had to make changes within myself to prepare for this calling. Without maturity, I would be unable to handle my new standard of living.
Throughout my journey, I was concerned about the source of the required finances, resources, and guidance for entrepreneurship. The more I cleansed myself spiritually, mentally, emotionally, and financially, the more God aligned me with the right people to answer my calling. Frequent visions, dreams, and ideas were given to me, and becoming an author was the one that most frightened me. Recalling the portion of my story that I started writing in 2017, I put my faith and trust in God and finished developing my story.

Every time I tried to fulfill my dream on my own, I was met with defeat. Left to my own devices, I was unable to find a publisher and editor. When God connected me to my guardian angel, Charron Monaye, founder of Pen Legacy, LLC., she gave me much more than just a publisher.

I recall the first conversation I had with Charron. Honestly, I was nervous, timid, and a little skeptical. I was in disbelief. An author? No, not me! Becoming an author was just a dream. I never imagined it would be my reality. My story was more than just a dream; it was God's gift of grace to me. Although I knew God led me to Pen Legacy, I was still suspicious and apprehensive. Living in Washington, DC, and signing with a publisher in Philly meant we only communicated via telephone and email. I often thought it was crazy to take such a leap of faith. Although I did my research, I was still doubtful. Deep down, I knew it was given to me and therefore meant for me. Talk about crazy faith, I stepped out on an opportunity that I could barely fathom, much less see or touch. I stepped out of my shell and challenged myself to be a vessel of God's grace.

I picked the baton back up and launched Empower Too Inspire, LLC, where my mission is to inspire, empower, and embrace many to revel in their truth, purpose, and power. Encouraging others to embrace their vulnerability to heal and love themselves unapologetically, it has been a great success thus far. One thing I've learned through my journey is to be attentive to my needs and trust God's timing. Everyone has a time to shine, and now it's mine! My pastor told our congregation, "Don't allow time to rob you of your faith." I'm a living witness to this statement.

June 2019, I became a published author, releasing my first book titled *Confidence Unlocked*, and then co–authored *Get Out of Your Own Way Vol. 3* in October and *Speaking My Truth* in November. Who would've thought my thoughts and feelings would become a best-selling book in the Family and Personal Growth category on Amazon? In addition to my personal success, both co-author projects hit the bestsellers list! Who would've thought there was purpose in every calamity I faced? I really am strong, because I overcame and survived. My becoming an entrepreneur and author was God's way of taking control and ensuring that my future reflected His heart. The craziest part about it all is He's just beginning. I had to trust God's plan even when I didn't understand it, couldn't see it, was afraid of it, and wanted to quit it! I did it scared, and I did it well. With God, along with my dedication, commitment, and faithfulness, I will succeed. Because I didn't quit and had the courage to try again, I'm able to share my story freely without shame! So, when they ask me how I made it, the answer is always the same: "Faith."

Toni Moore, Esquire

Toni Moore, Esquire, is a Wealth Building Lawyer who empowers women to build wealth through entrepreneurship. During Toni's 20+ year career, she has worked as a mid-level law firm associate, as a financial fraud investigator, as a business owner, adjunct professor, mutual fund specialist, insurance agent and a "side hustler" for several MLMs. In her latter years, Toni is personally committed to empowering women to own their power to become who God created them to be.

Toni graduated from the University of Pennsylvania and Temple University Beasley School of Law. Toni Moore is a licensed attorney in the States of Pennsylvania and New Jersey, teaches nonprofit compliance and public policy, and previously maintained a PA/NJ insurance license, mortgage broker's license, and Series 6, 63, and 26 Investment Licenses. Toni is an active public speaker for women's retreats, children's ministries, and entrepreneurial boot camps. Toni is also the author of *Boss Up!: Upgrade Your Mindset to Uplevel Your Success; Sanctify Your Money: The 11th Commandment; Stop Being A Doormat & Start Being A Boss; Handle Your Business: Power Moves to Make Your Dreams a Reality* and a fellow co-author in *Get Out Of Your Own Way: Overcoming Adversity to Live In Your Truth Out Loud* and *Get Out of Your Own Way: 11 Game-Changing Stories on Mastering the Power of Trust, Faith & Success.*

Contact Info:
Social Media: @ MSToniMoore
Website: legallychic360.com or mstonimoore.com
Email: tonimoore@legallychic360.com.

Give Yourself Permission to Live Your Dreams

According to the statistics, I am deemed as an anomaly. I was born to a teenage mother who named the wrong man as my father. After my parents were divorced, she raised me as the daughter of another man who was abusive to her. Throughout the in-between, I not only survived the realities of my childhood, but I found a way to achieve more than what others ever expected of me. More specifically, before I reached the age of ten years old, I had run away, lived in public housing, other people's basements, in the foster care system, with my grandmother and family friends. While others got stuck in the realities of an impoverished life, something within me compelled me to believe that I was more than enough to live a life that reflected my dreams. Instead of giving in to my life experiences and circumstances, I began to study other people who shined in life. If they looked happy, rich or were living life on their terms, I began focusing on them. As I stopped focused on my life within the governmental restrictions or under the watchful eye of social workers, I began seeking and requesting opportunities to have, do and be more. Believe me, when I say it was hard trying to thrive in a life most barely survived. From living beyond food stamps, fostered experiences, abuse, and financial suicide, the likelihood of overcoming obstacles to make my dreams possible was hard. But what I know for sure, what you always get what you focus on.

During my sophomore year in high school, I had the chance to go to the Milton Hershey School. For the first time in my life, I was surrounded by a tribe of people who helped me become a better version of myself. During my short time at the Milton Hershey School, I lived a life opposite of what I had grown accustomed to. I didn't experience instable housing, food shortage, emotional distress, or physical abuse. The three-year escape from my reality gave me a chance to do what I loved and to be who I wanted to be. While a junior in high school, I was also allowed to study and visit colleges and universities. But when I was first allowed to visit college campuses, I never thought it was for me. I never thought I would go to college. No one in my family talked about college. And in truth, prior to my Milton Hershey School experience, I was fixated on becoming a hair dresser business owner that dated a drug dealer.

Thankfully, I had two teachers who begged me to apply to college. I was getting stellar grades and proving myself to being a student leader (after being ejected from two different student homes). I loved researching, arguing, and challenging authority, but I figured college could wait while I made money and lived far, far, far away from the poverty line relegated to girls like me. However, my focus on becoming a hair stylist changed during a career day presentation. I don't recall what I presented on as I was going through the motions. But after hearing another's presentation on what lawyers do, my soul shifted.

My focus on becoming a lawyer helped me t go beyond my realities. At home, there was trauma, abused, instability and poverty but at school I began to dream about being a lawyer. I began wondering what if I lived my dreams, what if I could get into college, what if I became a lawyer. The more I asked what could happen if I allowed myself to live my dreams, I started to dream again. When I wondered what life could look like if I was accepted into the University of Pennsylvania, I applied and was accepted into the school. When I imagined getting beyond academic probation (not once but twice), I did whatever I could to graduate. I stopped partying, stopped drinking liquor while doing school projects and stopped hooking up with male students who only wanted to make a hooker out of me. Before I knew it, I had made the Dean' list, became a Student Advisor and graduated from the University of Pennsylvania with a B average.

Before I became a lawyer, I saw myself as one who helped others reclaim their power to turn dreams into possibilities.

Once I graduated from Penn, I took a year off to rest my brain. Believe me when I say that it was not an easy feat turning a D-/F average into a B average. But it was necessary to ensure I didn't burnout and miss out on becoming a lawyer. Upon graduation from Penn, I began focusing on my dream life as a lawyer. With a handful of friends and a belief in myself, I gave myself permission to sacrifice for my dreams. I didn't have the financial support so I took whatever job I could to make ends meet. My experience as a law student became more comfortable when I discovered an opportunity to work as a graduate assistant.

Upon graduation from law school, I started my career as a law clerk to a judge in the Eastern District of Pennsylvania. I had dreams of becoming the Johnny Cochrane of my generation. So, I took a job that gave me a front seat to litigation. After my clerkship, I took a job at an insurance defense firm which dimmed my shine. Once I began working at the insurance defense firm, I began to question why I had chosen to be a lawyer. I didn't have a mentor to guide me but partners who always criticized me. Nor did I have a group of colleagues who were appreciative of my skin color or my gender. I found myself encountering something I could never have imagined in my dreams—racism, and misogyny in a professional setting. I naively thought that once I overcame poverty, my life would be better. I thought that once I earned my degrees, more doors would open up for me. I felt that somehow I would become an amazing person living happily ever after once I had overcome my childhood trauma and adolescent struggles.

After six months of billable hour madness, I went to networking even. I met an attorney who had an accounting background who worked as a financial planner. In less than thirty minutes, my focus shifted after learning that who he deemed as his wealthiest client was an older black woman who worked as a cleaning lady for the then Cheltenham Mall. This client of his saved up almost two hundred thousand dollars to create an endowment to help black girls go to college. Somehow, her story resonated with me. I realized that money didn't make a person, but people could make a difference with the money they earned. Almost six months after meeting the accountant, I left the insurance defense firm and started my own law firm.

I didn't know the rules of engagement when I first started my firm. But I wanted to help others discover what the older woman saw in herself, an opportunity to turn her dreams into realities. I had my own firm for about three years and then partnered with another law firm. While working with this firm, I had more resources to help more people create change in their life and business. While at the firm, I helped some people create and develop nonprofit organizations. I helped others create resolutions with family and small business matters. I helped others appreciate their ability to bigger, better and more dreams. And while my life at the firm was not a tale of 'happily ever after,' I found myself settling into a life that was better I had ever imagined.

After two of my sisters died as a result of domestic violence, and I almost died from medical negligence, another aspect of me rose up. About a year after my second sister died, I began advocating for women to find a way to live their happily ever after here on earth. Whether people were going through a bankruptcy, divorce, the death of a breadwinner, I did what I could to ignite a fire within others to live beyond their pain. In fact, my greatest passion is to see others pursue their version of 'happily ever after' on this side of heaven.

As a child, I would often hear, "You'll get your happiness, you'll get your jewels, you'll get your crown of joy when you die." But I don't believe that we have to wait until we die before we live a life we love. Life lessons and history have consistently shown me that other people have gone through their life experiences with less than I've gone through and made it. Many people have suffered far worse than me but found a way to turn their mess into happiness. In light of what I've gone through, what I've helped others go through, and what I know people have suffered in silence, I know we have what it takes to live better dreams. Unfortunately, when you stop believing, you stop doing and when you stop doing you stop becoming and when you stop becoming then you stop yourself from being who you were created to be.

Good, bad or indifferent, people will judge you and say that you got served what you deserved. People who know you might even say that if you really wanted something different, you would have done something different. Others might even say that if you really wanted to live your best life, you would have asked for more. In the alternative, they might even say that if you genuinely wanted to live happily ever after, you would have been intentional about making things happen. Similar to the fairy tales, our quest for living beyond our dreams begins with saying yes to opportunities that you could have never imagined. Once they said yes to follow a yellow brick road, going to the ball, fighting for their rights or living their dreams, life changed tremendously. Similarly, if you are going to slay your legacy in 2020 and beyond, you need to give yourself permission to live bigger dreams. Never count yourself out, but continually count yourself in no matter what happens.

Kinyatta E. Gray

Kinyatta E. Gray is an Author and the Creator & CEO of FlightsInStilettos®. FlightsInStilettos® was founded in 2018 by Kinyatta based on her real-life travel style -- traveling glamorously through the airport. Kinyatta's goal is to inspire women travelers to put their best selves forward when traveling and to think about their individual travel style. Since launching FlightsInStilettos, the signature t-shirts and travel accessories have been spotted around the world. "Travel, Glamour, Slay." In 2019, FlightsInStilettos® debuted during New York Fashion Week and was spotted being worn by a host of celebrities.

In addition, FlightsInStilettos was featured on noted top tier websites such as Buzzfeed and ThriveGlobal. FlightsInStilettos® has been worldly recognized by vast platforms. Rising in the brand's success, FlightsInStilettos was featured in Fashion GXD Magazine, which was advertised on Amazon.com and Barnes & Nobles. FlightsInStilettos was highlighted on the "Travel in Style" segment of BMORE Lifestyle on MyTV24 Baltimore co-anchored by Chardelle Moore & Christina Denny. Kinyatta released her first memoir in 2019 entitled: *30 Days: Surviving the Trauma and Unexpected Loss of a Single Parent as an Only Child.*

Contact Information:
Email: info@kinyattagray.com
Facebook: kinyattagraytheauthor
Twitter: @Fstilettos
Instagram: @kinyattagraytheauthor
Website: https://www.kinyattagray.com/

The Open Secret

When I was a little girl, I used to love the movie Annie. The idea that a little girl could go from rags to riches was mesmerizing and everything that transpired in that movie made me believe the same thing could happen to me. I was infatuated with that movie and didn't learn why until years later.

I grew up in the church; not just any church, but a stiff, strict unforgiving church. This church was so strict, it didn't let my mother have her wedding there, because she had me out of wedlock. My mother married my biological father when I was two years old in a private ceremony. Several years later, that marriage ended in divorce. My mom found what she thought was love again many years later and was engaged to be married a second time. When planning her 2nd wedding, she learned that the church she was committed to for many years, would not allow her to marry there, because she'd given birth to me before her first marriage. My stepdad and mom would eventually marry somewhere else; however, being ostracized in this manner left my mom and stepdad hurt and bitter and they soon left that church to settle in a new one.

During their marriage, I was instilled with strong Christian values and my mom thought it best to keep me busy by involving me in the children's choir and bible study. I was a bible verse-quoting champion and could quote bible verses backwards and forwards. Back then, all of the kids in church took pride in quoting scriptures, not because we thought it made us holy, but because we enjoyed the challenge of knowing scriptures that no one else did. These were the kinds of games "church kids" would play to pass time during long Sunday services. My mom also went to church during weeknights. They had so many different services that one could attend that I presumed, the more services you attended, you were perceived as more holy. On nights when my mom had choir rehearsal, I'd run around the church playing mostly innocent games with the little boys and girls in the church basement. Those were truly the good old days. Mama never knew I was running around in the church basement acting like a fool, LOL. I'd straighten myself up, smooth my ponytails down and sit in my chair sucking on a peppermint, just before it was time to go home. Mamma's perfect little *"Peach out of Reach"*.

Growing up, I was only exposed to one kind of family – consisting of one man, one woman and 2 kids. I don't recall my parents ever educating me that alternative families existed. I don't blame them – because it didn't exist in their world. As a child, I had no concept of homosexuality—never even heard of it. It never existed in my mind or thoughts (or at least so I thought) until I became a teenager and came in contact with a woman who was a lesbian. Let's call her *DC Gay Girl*. I now know her to be a lesbian, but when I met her – I found her to be sort of strange because she was significantly older than me – but yet, seemed to have some odd physical attraction to me. I saw her as someone cool and fun to hang out with and this was made easier because she always paid for everything, but I could neither understand nor comply with some of the things she would casually share that she wanted to do with me. I realize now, that I was being "groomed".   I didn't feel comfortable with her sexual suggestions and advances and ended the friendship.

The seed was planted and I was somewhat intrigued.
In high school, I experienced the same thing again. I was completing a high school nursing program when a woman befriended me. Let's call her *MD Gay Girl*. I was very interested in this friendship because MD Gay Girl worked in the medical field, and since I was pursuing nursing, I felt that this was a great way to connect with someone who could help me get my feet in the door. I considered this to be a friendship made in heaven. Our friendship quickly blossomed and I enjoyed spending time with MD Gay Girl. She wasn't much older than me, but certainly old enough to have an apartment and transportation. Once my guards were down and I began to trust her, she began to talk to me about same sex relationships.   This time, I wasn't quiet as "green" or

unexposed, since DC Gay Girl had previously exposed me to the same kind of energy that I was now feeling from MD Gay Girl. The difference this time was that I was older and found MD Gay Girl's introduction to an alternative lifestyle rather interesting and I accepted it.

The seed was watered and started growing.
Without having yet come to terms with my sexuality and still rather confused as a teenager, I entered into a long-term heterosexual relationship. By the time I was 24, I left that 7-year abusive relationship after meeting a Spitfire Latina who worked in the Death Care industry. While toxic, two of the most beautiful beings were created, my son and daughter. I felt that energy again in the air from the Spitfire Latina that I had felt before when I was younger with DC and MD Gay Girl. This time, unlike the times before, I was open to engaging in a full fledge **secret** relationship with her. I could count on one hand the number of people I shared this secret with - one being my mom, because I told her everything.

I chose not to share information about my relationship, because by this time, I had been in the workforce and had been privy to the water cooler talk that included hurtful jokes, bias and discrimination of gays and lesbians. Same sex relationships were frowned upon in the circles I traveled in. In my mid-20s, my friends were getting married to their longtime boyfriends and settling in their 3-bedroom apartments with their kids. I wanted to fit into that narrative of what life was supposed to be. I wanted to fit in at work and not be ostracized for whom I loved. So I secretly blended into a heterosexual world, except I was lesbian.

Note: Unless you are positive about a person's sexual orientation and or family status, do not assume that you know someone's sexual orientation based on their appearance. Quite a few bigots revealed themselves to me simply because they made assumptions about my sexual orientation. I always "checked" people when they made disparaging comments, but fell short of telling them about me.

I blended into that world because of my attractive and extremely feminine outer appearance. In slavery days, super fair skinned black people who could easily blend into white society because of their complexion were accused of "passing" as white. Using that same analogy, because of my beauty, demeanor and feminine ways, I passed as heterosexual in the workplace and society as a whole. Whenever someone would engage me about love and relationships, I would refer to my partner using pronouns such as "they" or lie altogether and refer to her as "him" or "he". Passing as "straight" or hetero had its advantages. Men adored me, which made my life a whole lot easier. I worked my feminine charm to get what I needed, but I never disrespected or misled anyone in the process. I was always considered rather elusive and people loved the mystique surrounding me – because again, I was that "Peach out of Reach". As time went on, I started to feel frustrated and stressed out having to love in the dark and in the proverbial "closet". I never went on double dates because my date would have been a woman and I didn't want to be exposed.

During this "open" secret relationship, I experienced what I thought I would never experience once I left that 7-year relationship. Spitfire Latina was smitten with me, a 20-something hot and sexy young thing taking a liking to her. There was just one problem – Spitfire Latina had not properly ended a long-term relationship she was involved in with a woman who was old enough to be my mother. Yup! I found myself in a motherfucking lesbian love triangle. I went from being in a relationship with a man who cheated on me with women who I'd maliciously pursue since they were the object of his affection, to be the object of malicious pursuits by a scorned 40 year-old lesbian! Having only experienced dysfunctional relationships, the drama was familiar to me; the energy associated with lies, cheating and deception was familiar to me – so I didn't immediately run from it – I engaged it. Sometimes I even found it amusing since I was never the type to back-down from a little competition. After engaging in endless fights and witnessing the ruthlessness of a scorned woman, I decided I wanted more for my life and my children. I knew that I was never going to get that with Spitfire Latina. In spite of all of the drama, there was one thing that had become crystal clear – I was indeed a lesbian, but she was not worth me exposing my secret life.

In 2004, that would all change one night after I met a woman (who would become the love of my life) at a mutual friend's milestone birthday party. I was hanging out with my BFF at the time and she was the best --she knew of my secret life and she'd try her best to support me. We'd make agreements that if I went to the popular straight clubs with her that she'd go to gay clubs with me. That night, it was her turn to support me and she accompanied me to the birthday party. Let's call my new love interest "Wifey". Wifey and I engaged in a world wind romance that swept me off my feet. She wasn't completely single when we met and was in process of ending a dead end relationship with someone straight. Crazy, right?

When I learned of this, I gave Wifey an ultimatum. I said you have two weeks to get her and her shit out of your house or I'm done. I had learned from experience not to let this kind of situation linger. Two weeks later, Wifey called me and let me know that she was unattached and I was all hers. That was the first time that someone made me feel like a priority. Someone chose my two children and I – something I had never experienced. The love between us grew exponentially over the years. We developed trust, a sense of security; she made me feel safe and we knew we wanted to settle down together.

Oddly enough, she was accustomed to being a "secret" because she dated women who identified as "straight". Yup! There are tons of "down low" women just like "down low" men – they just receive less press. But this time was different; I didn't want her to be a secret. I didn't want my life to be a secret. I was tired of hiding my life, looking over my shoulders to make sure no one I knew saw us out a dinner, avoiding certain events in fear of who would see us together. My biggest fear was always being "ousted" by someone I worked with, but it was now *time for a change*.

In 2017, that change would finally come. After 13 years of a committed and loving relationship (having experienced love, joy, safety and security like I had never known), Wifey and I were married in a lavish wedding amongst family and friends who were in our super small inner circle. Around this same time, I was scheduled to start a new job. During the 13 years of our dating, no one in my place of employment knew of my secret relationship. If anything, most assumed I was either single or simply dating – but in reality, I was madly in love with Wifey. Because I loved and valued Wifey so much, I decided that once I started my new job that my life and whom I choose to spend it with would no longer be a secret.

We both exhaled.

She would no longer have to be someone's dirty little secret and I could live my life openly and unapologetically. I learned that families come in many different combinations and that at the end of the day, everyone has the same need and yearning for love and acceptance. We just wanted to raise my 2 children together in our home, maybe get a dog and live out our days peacefully. Now back to why I loved the movie Annie -- I was infatuated with Anne Reinking (Daddy Warbuck's secretary in the original Annie movie made in 1982) because she spotted unloved and unwanted Annie at the orphanage and saw the absolute best in her; she specially selected Annie to love, and to live a life of luxury with a billionaire, which resulted in Annie living the life of her dreams. Well, I may not have ended up with the material riches of a billionaire, but I ended up finding riches of the heart by being spotted, selected, loved and eventually settling into a fairytale lifestyle with the families of my dreams – just like orphaned Annie.

Tinesha Boswell

Tinesha Boswell was born and raised in Philadelphia, PA and she is a wife, mother, Motivational Speaker, Wellness Coach, an aspiring author. Tinesha has a Bachelor of Science in Business Management degree from University of Phoenix. She is also a Certified Life Coach, Marriage Mentor Coach and is currently studying Nutrition and Aromatherapy. Tinesha is also the founder of i.P.U.S.H Wellness Coaching and Consulting LLC.

What lead her to create i.P.U.S.H is due to her multiple chronic illnesses; asthma, high blood pressure, high cholesterol, type II diabetes, and fibromyalgia. Its purpose is to help you become at peace with your illness by learning to how to best deal with your chronic illness. i.P.U.S.H Wellness mission is to help women PUSH pass their pause by teaching them how to balance their Mind through personal development, their Body with fitness and nutrition, and by creating peace and Tranquility in their lives.

Contact Info:
Website: www.itsyourbodyyourtemple.com
Email: Tinesha@ipushwellness.com
All Social Media: Tinesha Boswell
Business Line: 267-209-0144
Cell: 267-428-8005

The Power of Our Senses

Growing up, I would always hear my parents complain about their jobs and how backwards their bosses were. They used to complain so much to the point that it made me not want to work for anyone...ever. However, it was a lesson that I needed to realize on my own. I got my first job when I was 14 years old (working at the Penn State College in Philadelphia), tutoring younger kids. I learned how to float and swim backwards (don't ask me to do it today because I haven't done it in so long) and learned how to control a room full of kids. That was my first real job, and I had a ball!

Fast forward to 2007, I started my first networking marketing business as a Travel Agent, which I am still one today. While working with other coaches in the field, the one thing they train you on is working hard. The saying was, "I will sleep when I die!" and I lived by this motto for a long time. I would work a full-time job, take care of my kids, and get travel quotes for clients after I put my kids to bed. Some days, I wouldn't see my bed until 3 am; and then had to get up at 5 am to start my day. I would always remind myself that it's okay because I have goals, and I can't achieve them if I am sleeping. However, working like crazy and getting only 2-3 hours of sleep a day was for the birds! I was always tired, irritable, and I wasn't a charming individual to be around when I was exhausted, which didn't stop me until one night I was so exhausted, I could do anything BUT sleep.

I didn't realize that *being* an entrepreneur meant a ton of stress, sleep deprivation, more health problems, especially mental health. It wasn't until devastation hit my door that I had to tell myself that this cannot be it. I can't believe that all successful people are stressed and not having any fulfillment in their businesses. As a Health and Wellness coach, I should have known better than to live like this because I knew that physical/mental health is vital to our well-being.

It all started in 2017 when things in the house began to break; and on top of all that, my son was arrested for being a suspect for murder. Our heater broke and had to be replaced, which costs a few thousand dollars. Did I mention that we didn't have any credit cards and had very little savings? We had to use what little we had and use the money allocated for our mortgage and bills to get it fixed. We didn't have much of a choice since our kids still lived at the house, and physically, I couldn't live in a cold house due to my fibromyalgia. Oh, by the way, we had a pretty bad leak in our bathroom that we couldn't get fixed because of the broken heater.

Well, eventually the living room ceiling got so wet that it collapsed, which meant we had no choice but to get it fixed. Meanwhile, we are trying to play catch up with our bills. We were paying our bills, but we were so far behind that it was hard to get caught up. Eventually, we went into foreclosure, which caused more stress.

During all this, my husband started having problems at work that resulted in stress leave. After being out on stress leave for a few months, it gave him anxiety on the mere thought of *going* back there to work, so he quit his job in January 2019 and became an entrepreneur by using Lyft as his primary source of income. All of this was happening while in court for the house. In February 2019, the judge granted us a repayment option and put what we owed on the back of the loan. Because he left his job, he had access to his 401k, which helped us get caught up on all our bills, and he helped me get a car since I was taking the bus.

Mom was losing weight rapidly, and the doctors had no clue what was happening to her. Mom went from 109 lbs to 60 lbs in a matter of months. It was extremely difficult to watch my mother wither away right before my eyes. Talk about stress, depression, and being mentally unstable! This was a very challenging time for us. However, I still had to work at my full-time job and work my business. Well, yet again, my business took a hit because I was too unstable to operate it properly. Then the evitable happened, mom passed away on August 16th, 2019, and 4 days later (August 20th) dad had a nearly fatal car accident and woke up in the hospital. We had to go against doctor's order and had him released from the hospital because he had to be at the funeral home on August 23rd because the funeral was on the 24th. I nearly lost my mind but had to do my best to stay in control of the family. I didn't want them to see me break because I was known as the "strong one," and I had no idea what it meant to be vulnerable.

With everything happening, bills again got behind, and we ended up in foreclosure back yet again. Not to mention I lost my job in December 2019. Emotionally I was tapped out, and I wasn't sure what I was going to do. Due to the devastation that happened in the past few years, I decided it was time to seek therapy to help me through all my emotions. In my therapy sessions, I learned that as entrepreneurs, many of us are stressed beyond our limits but aren't doing what's necessary to take care of ourselves because we are so worried about being successful. Although I am a Wellness coach and I understand the importance of taking care of our mental and emotional health, I also know that we as **women** entrepreneurs put our families and businesses ahead of *us*.

I started doing more research on mental wellness as it pertains to entrepreneurship, and the numbers were overwhelming. According to a study by the University of San Francisco, researcher Michael A. Freeman found that approximately one half (49%) of entrepreneurs suffer from at least one form of mental health condition during their lifetimes (please see Reference **1**).

I know what you're thinking: Why is she telling me all of this? I'm so glad you asked!

Have you ever woken up, looked at the ceiling, and said to yourself, "Not today!" I know that I have said it a few mornings. It's incredible how you can feel good when you go to bed and then wake up feeling like crap. It can be for any reason and I know EXACTLY how you feel! I wake up in pain throughout my entire body almost daily, and talk about back pain, ugh, I could scream sometimes! I was very stressed out to the point that I get migraines. Well, I have suffered from all the stress symptoms that you read above.

But as an employee, a mom, wife, sister, and business owner, etc., I felt I had to suck it up and keep it moving. When I started my mental therapy sessions, I learned (the hard way) that it was best for me to *un*-learn all that I had learned up to that point about mental awareness. You may be asking yourself right now, "What do you mean?" As a Mental Health Advocate, you learn all different types of techniques to deal with others who are suffering from poor mental health (whether minor or major), but don't always use the training on *yourself*. I had to allow my therapist to work with me and through me without me saying; I know that already.

I was struggling with the death of my mother, and most days, it takes me at least 10 minutes to get myself together, so I use that time to pray in the morning. I thanked God for waking me up that morning and the ability to feel because I know that someone, somewhere, did not make it. I had to show extreme gratitude for my life because tomorrow is not promised to anyone.

I had to PUSH myself, and it wasn't an easy task. PUSH simply means to keep going when everything in your body is telling you to quit. When God gave me the name PUSH, I didn't realize that it would help me through my mom's transition. Because I am still a mom, wife, grandmother, daughter, entrepreneur, etc., I needed to relearn how to **P**ersevere, I needed to know that I was **U**nique, I knew that I needed help. Hence, **S**olidarity is what I searched for, and I needed to regain **H**ope in my life.

To *slay your legacy*, you must find time to take care of your mental, physical, emotional, and spiritual well-being. You cannot allow your circumstances to take over your entire being like I did because it's not helpful to anyone and will cause you even MORE stress. I am now Soaring in my life and business!

Here's a little exercise that I have done (and still do) to help me through some of the challenges I have experienced and to make sure that I make time for self-care. I want you to think about your five senses, which are: touch, taste, smell, sight, and sound. Whenever you are having a stressful moment, I want to follow these steps and trust me, and you will feel less stressed than you were before you started the exercise.

An Act of touching
Our skin is the largest organ on our bodies and can be very sensitive to anything that affects the skin. You can use a lotion

that has a calming agent just as lavender to use on your hands while massaging it.

Taste of something Warm

Grab yourself some tea that can also be calming, such as Kava Stress Relief Tea by Yogi (please see Reference **2**). This is a "calming" tea that helps you to relax and find a sense of tranquility.

The power of smell

When you hear someone say, take a moment and smell the roses, while it's a bit cliché', it's very accurate. If you are at work, you can smell the calming lavender lotion that you massaged in your hand. When smelling the lavender, breathe in for four seconds from your nose, and breathe out for 4 seconds from your mouth. Repeat this process four times to feel peace and tranquil.

The imagination of your mind

Our minds can take us places we have never been because of our imagination. When you are stressed, think about where you would love to be in the moment. For me, when I am stressed, I visualize myself being on a beach, my feet in the sand cuddle up with a blanket and a good book. This has helped me in more ways than you can imagine!

Vibrations through sound

I like to listen to music when I am feeling stressed out and, most time, its musical jazz. You can use Spotify, YouTube, or iTunes to find a very soothing station. You can listen to the powerful sound of waves, rain, or bop to the beat of your favorite gospel artist. The goal is to listen to something that can help calm you.

Now I want you to think of how you can make this your own. You must be in the moment and mindful when doing this exercise and not allow anything or anyone to distract you. I would love to hear how it made you feel when you gave try it. Please email me at ipushwellness@gmail.com with your testimonials.

References:

1. https://www.weforum.org/agenda/2019/03/how-to-tackle-the-mental-health-crisis-in-entrepreneurship/
2. https://yogiproducts.com/teas/herbal-teas/kava-stress-relief/

Ontaria Kim Wilson

Ontaria Kim Wilson is a native of Philadelphia, PA. She has over 29 years in the entertainment industry. She began her journey with the world-renowned Rennie Harris Puremovement Hip Hop Theatre Company in 1991. She was a founding member and bid farewell to the company in 1997 to go on tour with R & B recording artist, Gina Thompson. She toured with Gina Thompson throughout the USA and Europe for a year. In 1998 she toured with Hip Hop recording Artist Eve as a background dancer and choreographer. While with Eve she was honored to perform on the following television shows: Soul Train, Show Time at The Apollo, NFL Under The Helmet, Motown Live, and The Conan O'Brien Show. Her next honor was choreographing and performing with the legendary Teddy Pendergrass. She toured with Teddy from 1999-2002 throughout the USA. She was honored to perform with Teddy in his last recorded performance "From Teddy with Love."

Ontaria's passion for dance thrusted her into the spiritual side of dance. In 1999 she became the dance ministry director for The Calvary Baptist Church of Philadelphia. During her tenure she became a dance ministry consultant for churches throughout the tri state area until 2015.

In 2013 she left her job at The Hospital of The University of Pennsylvania to pursue the arts full time. That year she began teaching performing arts to elementary school aged children and she wrote and produced her first stage play "THE HEALING." The Healing was her breakout production that confirmed her lifelong purpose of sharing the arts to touch one soul at a time.

In 2014 she wrote, produced, and directed her next staged brainchild "DETOX." Detox has transformed the lives of many people because of its message of healing the family by decreasing the use and power we give modern technology and social media. Detox has been in rotation for six years.

In 2018 she was a co-author in the Amazon Best Selling anthology "Bruised Broken & Blessed" published by Pen Legacy publishing. She also erected her third explosive stage production "BEAUTIFUL TOXICITY" which proved to be the catalyst for her first solo author experience. Because of the audience's request for more she converted the stage play into a book under the same title. Beautiful Toxicity was published by Pen Legacy publishing in 2019.

Ontaria is also an accomplished actress, director, screenwriter, certified life coach, and she holds an AA Degree in Theatre. Her mantra is "If God has downloaded a dream or vision into you it's your responsibility to complete the assignment. Someone is depending on your ``yes!''

Contact Information
Website: ontariawilsonllc.com
Email Address: info.ontariawilsonllc@gmail.com
Facebook: @ontariakimwilson
Instagram: @ontariakimwilson
Twitter @ontariakimwilsn

Know Your Purpose

When I was about three years old, my mother put me in an African dance ensemble. To this day I have a clear vision of my first performance. It was a hot summer day. I was dressed in a green and burgundy lapa with a matching top and head dressing. The beat of the drums urged me to dance around as if I was dancing a rites of passage ritual in the Congo. The joy I felt on the stage, dancing, and making people smile has remained with me for over forty years. Yes, it's been over forty years and the passion has grown into a full-blown career. A career path I was called and chosen to perform. It's more than a career, it's my life, my purpose.

Many people go through life trying to figure out what their purpose is. They dismiss those things they have enjoyed since they were children or those acquired interests they've accrued in their teen and adult years. Instead, they go on an insatiable quest for success based on what society associates with "true" success. They grasp for straws trying to find ways to become rich or the "next big star" without having a desire for the area of business they have chosen for themselves. They eventually find themselves in the never-ending rat race. They are unable to find gratification; they become stuck in a place where they see no way out; and they cast this mentality onto the next generation creating a perpetual state of "purposelessness." I don't mean in the sense of not having a desire to want better; but, in that they don't take the time to study themselves with the goal of finding out who they are, what they enjoy, or what things in life bring them fulfillment.

Okay, here's a moment of transparency. I'll be sharing a few of these along this journey. When I was in the twelfth grade, I was trying to figure out what I wanted to do after graduation. I thought of four different majors to choose in my college consideration. I had been told to make sure that whatever major I chose, to make sure it would lead to a lucrative career. Well, at that age I wasn't sure of the college, my major, or what would be lucrative. I just knew I wanted to dance and perform. I was encouraged to join the military because there I would receive "good benefits", a college education, and blah blah blah. I laughed and said, "I am too much of a free spirit to be put under someone else's control." I decided to go to a community college, but I was undecided in my major. I tried criminal justice because I considered social work. I tried accounting because I heard accountants make good money. I hated it! Then I tried speech communications. Nope, that wasn't it. During this time, I was in the honors program, working full time as a security officer, and a full-time performer with my dance company, Rennie Harris Puremovement. I was overachieving. But something happened. During finals week I had an anxiety attack. I stayed in bed the entire week crying, not speaking with anyone, and hoping that one day I would be able to ONLY do what I loved. My professors left voice messages for me to come and take my finals. They truly cared because we had formed a community and they knew that something was wrong. Needless to say, I didn't return. That was 1995. But I kept working and I kept dancing.

I went on to work at an alarm company, Universal Atlantic Systems. I became the assistant to the chief engineer. I was helping to close deals with major franchises around the country. I was flown out to meet with CEO's and loss prevention executives throughout the country as well. UAS was like family but it was my job. My real life started after 4:30pm. I was a choreographer and background dancer for The Legendary Teddy Pendergrass. I was also the choreographer for a gospel choir, TMJC. Both Teddy and TMJC were actively performing and touring during this time. I forgot to mention that I was the director of the dance ministry at my church. Yes, I stayed busy but I loved every minute of it.

One day I went to work and was called into the president's office. As I was gathering my notepad and pen, I was pondering over the possible accounts he would want to discuss. I walked briskly to his office greeting my coworkers as I passed them. I walked into his office, closed the door, and sat in my normal seat. My boss was putting something away in his file drawer. He greeted me with a melancholy: "Hey O!" That was his term of endearment for me. "Morning Scott!", I said. He went on discussing the updates on our recent restructuring of the organization. In an instant he quietly resolved into the headrest of his black leather chair, took his glasses off, rubbed his face, and looked at me. He then said, "You have done a wonderful job and you have been a true asset for the company. But, I know where your heart is. As much as I don't want to do this…" he paused as tears fell from his face: "I don't want blood on my hands, so I have to let you go." Those words were sweet to my ears. I looked at him with a soft smile and said, "Thank you. Thank you for trusting me with your company, for working with me as I toured, and for being obedient to what God told you to do. Thanks for everything." We hugged and cried and I knew at that moment that Corporate America was not for me. On that date my purpose was confirmed! I toured for nine months not having to commit to an employer. I was in heaven!

II

Write The Vision & Make It Plain
After I was let go, my creative juices started flowing. I was having dreams and visions of future endeavors that all tied into the arts. I purchased a hot pink leather-bound notebook and started transcribing my thoughts onto paper. I would write out what I saw. I would draw pictures that correlated so that I could have a visual of what was to come. This was new for me. Before then, I was accustomed to dancing out the visions that I had in my head.

Then I took it to another level. I created a vision board. My vision board had actual images of those things I envisioned. Words and phrases that inspired me were posted to this once white canvas. The board was full of color, full of life, full of future ambition, and endeavors. Between my notes and my vision board I now had a springboard into what my future would look like. I woke up every morning to the sun shining it's rays and my vision board reminding me of the journey set before me, of which I was the master of.

All of us are given visions and dreams throughout our lifetime. Some dissipate into the sea of forgetfulness but there are others that resonate in our spirits. Overtime those visions and dreams resurface and grab our attention. They trigger our mind to start thinking of the possibilities. It's important that you give these thoughts the attention they deserve by acting on them; and the first step is writing it out. The bible gives us a tidbit of wisdom on how to start the process of executing your dreams and visions. Habakkuk 2:2 reads as follows: "Then the Lord answered me and said: "Write the vision and make it plain on tablets, that he may run who reads it." It tells us that when you decide to respond to what God is calling you to do, through your dreams and visions, it's important to write out the vision, organize your thoughts, then run with it!

III

Go For It and Kill Fear
I now understood the blessing in writing the vision and making it plain, and because of this newly found cognizance I felt compelled to set goals in effort to manifest those dreams

that I had laid out for myself. But, in my goal setting I ran into the masters of dreams deferred: doubt and fear. Yup! They reared their ugly heads throughout my journey. Doubt was a subtle little beast. It would whip out its short, forked like tongue and say things like: "you can't afford that' and "you don't have enough training."   It would encourage me to measure my success based on my peers perceived success. Then fear crept in and paralyzed me. When moments would present themselves for me to network and share my vision to people who could potentially move the vision forward, I was unable to speak on my own behalf. Fear, without a clear understanding of how, paralyzed me from moving. The revelation finally hit me...I was afraid of rejection and I was safe in my own world.

I was in church and my pastor started a series entitled Divine Connections. This was a life changing point in my life and career. There were two points that changed my worldview and propelled me into the person I've become today.

- All encounters with people are divine appointments. This is a reminder that each time you meet someone it's important to get to know them because they, or you, could be the catalyst for your next level.
- You are divine. Walking in your divine nature gives you a level of confidence to go for whatever you desire to achieve. It also works in removing fear from your consciousness; when you activate this power, you become unstoppable. The bible reminds us of this power when it says: "Greater is He that is in me than he that's in the world." To some people this may not

click; but when you believe the God of the universe lives in you there is no way doubt or fear can survive. There's a level of confidence that lets you know that you are great, powerful, and able to do anything you set your mind to!

When I grabbed hold of this school of thought a fire was ignited inside of me. No longer did I doubt my abilities. No longer was fear paralyzing me because I killed it! I came to believe that I was more powerful than fear. Understand that we give fear life. Fear can't live where it's not received! Get up, Get Out, Get What's Yours!

IV

Take Risks
Since I learned my purpose, how to write the vision and make it plain, and walk in my divine power I began to capitalize. My gifts began to make room for me. What does that mean?

When I gained confidence in my crafts (dancing, writing, acting, and directing) I allowed myself to be more visible, to execute my plans, and create a lane for myself not contingent upon what other people could do for me. I became a risk taker. I became much like the disciples of Jesus. When they each met Jesus they were going about their daily lives based on what they "knew to do to survive." Once he approached them with His vision they responded with a yes. Their "yes" would force them to leave what was familiar and take a step into the unknown. They were risk takers who saw a future brighter than what the world told them they could have and they were successful. Maybe not financially, but they made a mark on the world that impacted people for generations to come. Now that's legacy!

In 2013 I took a risk that would forever be my "Yes" moment. I left what would be my final dance with normal full time 9-5 employment at Penn Medicine. My transition out was a stage play that I wrote in homage to the Department of Radiation Oncology called THE HEALING. It was my very first stab at writing a play, executive producing, and co directing. I had said yes to my future. After that groundbreaking experience doors started opening that I would have never imagined. I've acted in over 20 plays; written and produced four plays; directed five plays; directed a film; written three screenplays; authored and co-authored a total of three books now; featured on a syndicated television show; and more keeps coming my way. I can truly say that I have been blessed being a risk taker; but it hasn't always been peaches and cream.

With all my success I have had failure and trials. I came to understand that failure and trial transformed me into the powerful woman, artist, and entrepreneur I am today. All the lessons learned yesterday became my wisdom for today.

V

You Can't Do It By Yourself
So, remember back in chapter one where I shared the fact that I hadn't gone back to school. Well, I realized that if I wanted to be the best of the best then I couldn't do it by myself. I needed help. I needed people who could assist me in securing solid knowledge. I realized that the acquisition of knowledge would ultimately enlarge the territory for me to walk in my

purpose. I did two things. I hired a coach, Charron Monaye, to help whip me into shape regarding my business and my brand. I also decided to go back to school and finally get my degree.

I'm glad that I didn't force a major because it would have thrown me off course. When I finally decided to go back and finish, I knew for certain what my focus should be because I had been living it my entire life. I chose theatre. The crazy thing is that all the credits I had acquired earlier on applied to my major. Some classes were substituted, and I was awarded other credits based on my life experience as a performer. This left me with only seven classes needed to graduate. I was asked to come back to the honors program, but there was no need because I was about to graduate. I was invited to join the National Honor Society of America, among other invitations. Needless to say, I was blessed beyond measure and if I had to do it over again, I wouldn't change a thing because it was all in divine order.

Obtaining a business coach and going back to school helped me to gain solid footing in my career path. For so long I was doing things my way and doing what I "knew to do." There's something beautiful that happens when you know how and the know-how of others merge onto the same space. You become a force à laquelle il faut compter! I will forever be a student of life and of my craft. The moment you stop learning is the moment you choose not to thrive.

VI

Work Your Business

Like most of us, I thought about and talked about the amount of time devoted to making someone else's business successful. We commit on average eight hours a day to our employers. They train us on how to do the jobs required to make their businesses successful. They set guidelines on how the business should be run. They prescribe your hours worked based on their needs. You meet the demands of the job daily and clock out when you have served your time. And then, you go right back the next day and do it all over again.

What if you devoted just as much time, if not more, to your vision...your business...your future: eight hours a day, forty hours a week, fifty-two weeks in a year. Can you imagine the progress you could make in one year if you dedicated that amount of time to your dream? Now, I know some of you would say: "but that's not realistic." To some degree that may be true. Some of us need to have a regular 9-5 to supplement our households and our dreams. But if that is the case, you still need to structure the amount of time you devote to yourself. Even if it's three hours a day, fifteen hours a week, twenty weeks in a year...DO IT! Discipline yourself because no business can work without structure.

My success is contingent upon my investment in myself. I took back my time and committed to treating my dreams and my business like the business it is. I set hours for me to work. I implemented parameters regarding my business structure and how I executed my business. I recognized my value and began to charge accordingly for my services. I used to wear T-shirts and other paraphernalia that identified with my employer. Now I identify solely with my purpose, my dreams, and my future. I have branded my name, my business and I am fully committed to slaying and maintaining my legacy! I still have a lifetime to slay!

Keisha Griffin

Keisha Griffin is a Personal Development Strategist and Coach who designs her services to allow each client to gain greater levels of perception through personal development. Vision board workshops and coaching to design a better life, live with abundance while building amazing relationships. Keisha is a wife and mother who has experienced a series of joyful events and unfortunate opportunities in her life that have shaped her passion for helping women. She has persevered through depression, physical health challenges, career changes and an ever-changing family dynamic, Keisha is focused on building relationships and making a difference on purpose. With over 20 years' experience as a business leader, Keisha is a certified coach, speaker and trainer with The John Maxwell Team. Keisha has also completed training with Wellcoaches and the YMCA. Keisha has a Bachelor of

Arts in political science from Montclair State University and a master's degree in public administration from Keller Graduate School of Management. She has presented talks and facilitated workshops at corporate and small businesses, colleges, universities and nonprofit organizations. In 2019, Keisha founded Envision Quest Coaching that provides a unique range of virtual and in person services including one-one coaching, small group workshops and webinars that are interactive, motivational, engaging and designed to achieve results. Keisha's signature service is the Envision Board Experience, a curated personal development workshop that takes the vision board party to the next level. Contact Keisha to facilitate an event for your group.

Contact Information:
Business Website: envisionquest.coach
Business Email: envisionquestcoaching@gmail.com
Facebook: @envisionquestcoaching
Twitter: @envision_quest
Instagram-Business: @envision_quest
Instagram-Personal: @_keishagriffin

A Quest For Purpose

My name is Keisha Griffin, a life coach and personal development specialist. I am a wife, mother, and the CEO of Envision Quest Coaching, as well as a certified coach with The John Maxwell Team. I help my clients define a clear individual path through the process of building vision boards and coaching. My legacy began in North Carolina with parents, Gene Pridgen and Lou Myrtle Steele, who lived just miles apart yet seemingly were unaware of each other and their shared destiny. My mother, Lou Myrtle, was known as Cat by her family and close friends due to her fear of the vile creatures. When she came to New Jersey, her nickname became Pat. She was the oldest of three. My father, Gene, was the oldest of six. Both carried their roles as the oldest siblings with pride and strength, protecting and caring for their families as they built one together. It was the Jim Crow Era, where racial segregation prevailed as the way of life. To escape the harsh realities of the American south, they migrated north. However, it wasn't until years later that Gene and Pat would cross each other's path.

The youngest of four children, I was the sassy, little sister known for saying too much and usually at the wrong time. My brother, Darrin, and two sisters, Regina and Angie, were charged with keeping an eye on me. My father, who was an entrepreneur, owned and operated Gene's Refrigeration, an HVAC business. My mother was a stay-at-home mom until I started kindergarten. Then, she worked for the Elizabeth Public School System as a bus aide and classroom assistant until her retirement. We lived on the 2nd floor of a three-family house owned by my parents. I grew up in a large extended family with more aunts, uncles, and cousins than I could count, let alone name. Surrounded by loving people and positive vibes, I had a good childhood, of which I cherish the memories.

When I was a child, the infamous question, "What do you want to be when you grow up?" was heard over and over, and often in my parents' backyard. I felt the expectation of figuring out who I was and what I wanted to do. The truth is, I didn't know what I wanted to do with my life. But, I knew who I wanted to be, and that was a person who helped people and made a difference in the world. I wanted to do something fun and creative that would help me make a living and have a good life. Ever since I was a little kid on Anna Street, my vision for my life has been to build a legacy of service and make a difference on purpose.

Around 2005, Oprah Winfrey started telling the world to "Live Your Best Life." At the time, it sounded great, but I had no idea what it truly meant. I was a married, 32-year-old mother of two kids, ages four and six, just trying to get a good night's sleep for myself. I immersed myself in being a mom. So much so that I forgot about taking care of myself. I was a wife and mother before anything else.

It was during this phase of my life that I underwent a series of diagnostic tests and discovered I had a tumor in my pancreas. The doctors were baffled by my diagnosis because this usually only happened to older Caucasian men, not African American women in their thirties. However, the doctors quickly responded with a plan to remove the tumor within a few weeks of my diagnosis. The tumor was malignant but low grade. So, I did not require additional treatment. I never referred to myself as having the "C" word because I refused to claim that as part of who I am. This diagnosis was an unfortunate opportunity that helped to change my focus in life. It was the beginning of a journey to redefine my destiny. I focused on recovering so I could get back to my young family. I wanted to make health a priority and continue to live my best life.

At the time of my diagnosis, I was working for the county government as a business analyst. It was a job that I was good at but did not love. When I returned to work, I felt an overwhelming sense of depression and anxiety about my professional path. I was healthy again, but I knew that time would be short if I didn't make some changes. So, I decided to change my career from county government employee to a professional director at the YMCA, a non-profit organization focused on building healthier lifestyles. I was surrounded by people focused on community and purpose-driven change. As a YMCA professional, I had the opportunity to create programs designed to help individuals improve their health and well-being. I worked closely with community partners, local leadership, and my fellow YMCA professionals to build a safe, nurturing environment for kids, adults, and families. My time at the YMCA was a crucial part of my physical and mental healing process. I have since moved on to a career in higher education where I have the opportunity to guide and interact with a young, optimistic generation of students. As a higher education professional, I am in a position of service to others in a positive, professional environment that supports my overall health and well-being goals.

Over the past few years, I have devoted myself to health, wellness, and personal development. I have read countless books and attended workshops on the topic of empowerment. I became a self-development "junkie". Although I was consuming information on how to become my best self and live my life, I needed more personal accountability to achieve my goals. So, I wrote down my goals in a journal, but I still didn't follow through. I worked with a coach, but sometimes I needed more. That's when I began to envision how I wanted my life to look and who I wanted to be in 30, 60, 90 days, and five years. I discovered vision boards and used them as a way to compile my goals in one place that I could look at each day. Facing my goals each day made them realistic and tangible. My vision boards are a reference to remind me of what I want, who I want to become, and the steps I need to take to get there.

Vision boards have become a regular part of my self-care routine. I have found that the process of building a vision board is therapeutic.

In 2019, I decided I wanted to share the benefits that I gained from vision boards and coaching. My goal to help others and live with purpose manifested into Envision Quest Coaching, a curated experience of workshops, events, and coaching services designed to help women develop a vision for their lives. The Envision Quest Workshop is more than a vision board party with magazine cutouts. Envision Quest is my way of empowering women by helping them to focus on themselves for an hour or more during our sessions. Our workshop stands out as an experience that includes group coaching and self-reflection exercises. My one-on-one coaching services help women find realistic solutions to everyday challenges, self-care, and creating lasting relationships. Envision Quest Coaching will host purpose-driven trips to national and international destinations regularly. The vision I have for these curated trips will be to transform the destinations and experiences on each client's vision board into a reality.

As someone who has overcome the big "C", I am driven to live my best life unapologetically. Like many women, I wear many hats. In my 9-5 as a higher education professional, I help build influential, educated global citizens. My side hustle as a coach and CEO allows me to help women find their way back to who they are. I have been married for over 21 years, and my relationship is a testament to love, compromise, and communication. As a mother, we can be critical of ourselves for not being enough or doing enough for our children. I have been guilty of both. However, I know I have raised two amazing adults who are living the lives they have designed for themselves. I am a wife, married for over 20 years to a great man. As a wife, mother, coach and lady boss, I want my legacy to be defined by making a difference on purpose.

Teraleen R. Campbell

Teraleen R. Campbell is a native of Hagerstown, Maryland and currently resides in the Washington, DC metropolitan area. She is an award-winning author and speaker. In addition to serving in the ministry, she is a certified coach. One who knows the worth of prayer, Teraleen loves to intercede for others. She serves as lead intercessor each month for the Sisters Prayer Circle which is sponsored by Sisters 4 Sisters, Inc.

She became a member of Zeta Phi Beta Sorority, Inc. at the University of Maryland, where she conducted her undergraduate studies. She has numerous leadership positions in the organization, previously serving on serving as National Co-Director of Marketing. Her ministry extends to Zeta, as she now serves on the International Interfaith

Team. Teraleen authored the sorority's Centennial Prayer, has facilitated the Global Day of Prayer and co-authored the Faith of Our Founders Devotional Book.

Her community involvement includes the Prince George's County March for Babies Committee and Maryland Legislative Agenda for Women. She is Immediate Past President of a local club for Toastmasters International. Teraleen is a tireless advocate against domestic violence, engaging elected officials, supporting survivors, conducting workshops and sitting on panels that address this issue. Southern Management Corporation, the March of Dimes and the American Red Cross have recognized her for her involvement and service to the community. Additionally, she was named Sorority Woman of the Year during the annual Sister-to-Sister Sorority Luncheon, hosted by Taylor Thomas of WHUR Radio. She also was recognized by her sorority, having been inducted into Zeta's Maryland State Hall of Fame in 2016. She was named one of the DC Metropolitan area's 100 Phenomenal Women in 2015. She is a contributing author of Behind the Scenes of a Phenomenal Woman, and Confessions of a Caregiver which were released in 2018 and 2019.

With Christ as her focus, friend and guide, Minister Campbell's earnest desire is to be a vessel fit for the Master's use. (2 Timothy 2:21)

Do You Boo!!!

What is a legacy? If you're like me, you did not grow up hearing that term very often, if at all. Legacy defined - anything handed down from the past, as from an ancestor or predecessor.

For many of us when we consider our family histories and what has been handed down to us, they aren't exactly what we would consider to be stellar legacies. In many cases, handing down anything of a monetary nature was never part of the equation, not because our ancestors did not want to do so, rather because they did not have such resources. I have remembered that as an African American woman, I was born a few generations outside of slavery and Jim Crow to a single mother before being in such a category was accepted by society.

Despite all of that, my mother did establish her own legacy. That in turn served as the framework for mine. It's ironic how age and maturity enable you to appreciate the similarities that you share with your parents. Our commonalities include a legacy of service to others, a passion for prayer and interceding on behalf of others, investing in others (mentorship), and the ability to overcome the lemons that have been thrown at us in life. The most accurate word is fortitude.

As I process the life and death of the great Kobe Bryant, (yes, I am a sports fan,) I think of legacy.

My mind begins to ponder the question, what will we leave behind? People talk about him being one of the greatest to ever play basketball. They remember his prowess on the court. They mention the points that he scored. Some debate about Kobe versus Lebron and which are the greatest of all time, the GOAT if you will.

Then the conversation shifts. I have a revelation. Basketball is what got him in the door, it got the conversation going. It put his name out there and on people's minds. However, after Kobe left the court, the subject of the conversation was less about basketball itself and more about what he was doing with his life. It was about him being a wonderful father of four girls, him being a father and husband, who made some youthful mistakes but kept his family together and enjoyed life with them. He was a man who transitioned from one career into a life that he was excited about, which included coaching his daughter as she played the game that he loved.

He wrote children's books and made history by winning an Academy Award for a film that he produced.

Then I thought of my legacy.

While I may never be a millionaire and that's alright, I still have a legacy. If you are reading this, you have one too. The question becomes what will my legacy be? The question now becomes, what is it that I will leave behind? We all have to answer that question.

After my name has left the lips of others, what will be the lasting imprint that I have left behind? What is it about me that will outlive this mortal body? As I pondered these questions within myself, I shifted to the scripture where Jesus asked the man, "what do you have in your hand?" What do you have in your hand? So, I'm asking the Lord and this becomes my prayer as I work to *slay my own legacy* - Lord help me to use the things that you have placed in my hands to your glory so that they will impact others after I am gone.

Kobe is gone but the lasting footprints, the images, the things that he did in the community, opening a school, investing in young ballers, donating one million dollars to the African American History Museum so that our people's story could be told, being a doting girl dad is part of his legacy. Now we have to decide and walk out what will be our legacy. At 41 years of age, it's undeniable that Kobe left quite a legacy. Now we must put in the necessary work in order to establish ours. One thing that I know for sure is that building a positive legacy includes facing past hurts and taking steps the necessary to heal. We simply cannot focus on others while working to move forward in our lives. This may mean that it will be necessary to step away from people, places and things.

Step away, in other words – walk, but don't run. Sometimes God will use our struggles to set us up for something much greater. Be clear about how you expect to be treated and loved. Once you realize that you are not being treated according to the standards that you have established then you have an obligation to yourself to deal with the situation and course correct.

Course correcting may mean getting off of an emotional rollercoaster that is hindering your forward progress. This may include family, romantic, platonic, or professional relationships. The hard truth is that toxic relationships are sending too many among us into hospitals and early graves. Moreover, they are causing anxiety, depression and a myriad of other emotional disorders that hinder our ability to move in purpose and slay our legacy.

One thing I yet appreciate about my mother is that although my father left her just a few months after I was born, she never wasted energy telling me a bunch of negative things about him. No! She faced the situation as a 20-year old mother of a newborn, dealt with her broken heart and moved on. She did not allow that situation to make her bitter.

I too had to deal with the fallout from their failed relationship. Unlike the Bryant girls, I never knew my girl dad. In fact, I had to deal with the harsh reality that my father had opted to remove himself completely from my life. It took me years, well into my adult life, but I got to the point where I had to release the anger that I felt toward him. I did not do it for him – I did it for me. I chose not to use my emotional capital on someone whom I had never met in person. I also did not want my anger to carry over into relationships with other men. Likewise, it is critical that we use our failures and hurts to learn lessons, chart a new course and move on – *better, not bitter*. We owe that to ourselves and to those who will come along after us.

Once we free ourselves from toxic situations, we often will able to more clearly answer the question of what is in our hands that we can use.

Legacy is what we are working toward, it is ongoing and yet to be revealed. One thing is clear, we all have one. Second, copy cats are not allowed. Our legacy must be unique to us. It will reflect the work of our hands. It is not about anyone else, their dreams or their desires. It is about the dynamic person that we have been called to be and the great works that we are to put forth in this Earth.

Do not compare yourself with others to determine how well you are doing. You must be mindful that success comes in many forms. Everything is not always as it seems. Comparing yourself to others could render you a public success, but private failure. Be authentic, realizing that the only competition you have is with yourself and that is to be a better version of you as you grow and mature. Best believe that legacy slayers have overcome much. As Langston Hughes wrote, "life ain't been no crystal stair."

I was informed during the fall of 2018 that the company where I had been employed for 26 years would be eliminating my department in January 2019. The notification came just one week prior to the release and launch of my first solo book *From Carefree to Caregiver*. Needless to say, I dealt with a variety of emotions that included sadness, a tinge of fear and depression and even a sense of relief, as the past seven years had involved a great deal of change and loss for me.

It was during that period that I outlined goals that were important to me and aligned with my purpose. I realized that prior to the downsizing experience I had lost part of myself to the corporate world. As a result of being downsized, I vowed that although I would maintain a stellar work ethic, I would not spend so much energy building another person's wealth and legacy. I make this statement, not being arrogant. I now have a new awareness of what God has placed in my hands. I now realize that it would be irresponsible of me if I were to bury rather than use the gifts and talents that He has given me. I am also more aware than every that God does not give us gifts and talents for solely for ourselves. He also grants them to us for the purpose of us utilizing them as tools to bless and enhance the lives of others.

My parting word is by all means, do you!! Just remember, whatever you do and however you do it, you have got to own it, all of it. Own the triumphs, the challenges, and in between.

Own your life's race and give it all that you've got. Your name and your stamp will be part of it forever.

A good name is more desirable than great wealth. Respect is better than silver or gold. Proverbs 22:1 GNT

Barbara E. Allen

Barbara E. Allen is a Christian woman, who loves the Lord. She is: a native of Philadelphia, Pennsylvania with strong family roots in North Carolina, the proud mother of Donald Allen, Columbia, MD and Derrick Allen, Claymont, DE, and a member of Seeds of Greatness Bible Church, Newark, Delaware under the leadership of Pastor Jerome Lewis.

Barbara holds a BS in Elementary Education and a MS in Health Education from St. Joseph's University in Philadelphia, PA. As her thrust for knowledge of God and religion increased, she decided to attend Biblical Theological Seminary in Hatfield, PA where in 2005 she received a Master of Divinity in Leadership. Barbara has a love for teaching. This gift has been manifested in her role as a public-school administrator, teacher, director of women's and outreach evangelism ministries, and women's retreat/conference speaker. She has had the opportunity to teach the Word of God in Montego Bay, Jamaica, and Aklavik, Northwest Territories, Canada and do mission work in Ghana, West Africa. Barbara is the founder of Rinnah Worship Ministries. Rinnah is Greek for "proclamation" and her ministry seeks to proclaim the Good News of Jesus Christ and bring women to the knowledge of God through a retreat-style atmosphere. Above all that can be said or written about Barbara Allen, she simply wants to be known for being a disciple of Jesus Christ, the living Savior, and for joyfully committing her life to being obedient to the Will of God. Her life verses are Romans 8:35-39.

Igniting the Faith of the Believer

"Faith is taking the first step even when you don't see the whole staircase." ~Martin Luther King, Jr.

Ten, nine, eight, seven, six, five, four, three, two, one … Happy New Year! Every year at 12:00 a.m. on January 1st, millions of people celebrate bringing in the New Year. Whether they are at an elaborate formal gathering, joined together in a home with family and close friends, nestled on an island getaway, or in church praising and thanking God, people are excited about igniting their faith in regards to what the New Year will bring. For me, the latter has become my experience for over thirty years, because I love showing God how grateful I am for allowing me to see another year.

Now beside the various celebrations, comes the tradition of making that all too familiar New Year's resolution. I discovered that the origin of this whole New Year's resolution tradition started with the Babylonians. They would make promises to the gods hoping that they would earn favor in the coming year, often resolving to get out of debt. (Wikipedia.org) Today, we make promises with the intent of improving our lives for the upcoming year. We utilize our faith and trust that the things we have chosen as our resolutions will somehow manifest throughout the year. We ignite our faith to believe that we will lose weight, get out of debt, find a spouse, get a new job, quit smoking, buy a house, join the "Y", or volunteer at a hospital or senior citizen facility. Yes, our faith is renewed, and we are excited about what's going to happen. However, with all the excitement invested in the New Year, it has been researched that only eight percent (8%) of people achieve their goals (University of Scranton study, 2018). What happens, why does our faith dwindle, isn't faith believing in what we cannot see?

As a believer, I no longer make resolutions to begin the New Year. I noticed that every year they were pretty much the same promises and that I never really reached the eight percent status of folks who actually accomplished their goals. Instead, for the last three years I have chosen to participate in the Daniel Fast with my church family, kindling my faith to believe that God will answer prayers. The fast consist of voluntarily abstaining from eating specific foods for twenty-one days. This year we are also reading a chapter of the book of John every day, as well as the following suggested books, "The Power of I Am" by Joel Osteen, "If You Were God

Would You Choose You?" by Rick Renner and "Prayer Warrior" by Derek Prince. What a great plan for building your faith. "Faith consists in believing when it is beyond the power of reason to believe." Voltaire.

This year as we began our fast, my Pastor asked us to really think about the reason why we were fasting. Now, I won't lie. I had compiled a prayer list that quite frankly in some regards sounded a lot like my old resolutions. Let's see lose the weight (check), join the "Y" (check), financial freedom (check), need I go on? As I looked at my list, I felt that something was very wrong. Had I made God like some type of genie or Santa Claus? Did my list consist of a lot of stuff and things that I believed I deserved? Was adding prayer a way to make it all seem legit? Oh yeah, something was definitely wrong.

Now on the sixth day of the fast I was reading the sixth chapter of John. When I reached the twenty-ninth verse, I had a "ah-ha" moment. The verse read, "This is the only work God wants from you: Believe in the one he has sent." And just like that I recognized the reason for my fasting. It wasn't to present some giant shopping list to God and sit around waiting for Him to fulfill it. I had it all wrong! As I read John 6:29 (NLT) I realized that God's desire for me was to simply believe (have faith) in His son Jesus Christ. I got it! This meant that I had to determine in my heart, mind and soul that Jesus was my Source. All I needed to do was to stay connected by reading His Word and keep the faith. Oh yes, I needed, I wanted that Harriet-Tubman type faith.

Harriet Tubman was a great abolitionist who was renowned

for guiding her fellow slaves to freedom on the Underground Railroad. This year across the United States they featured a movie about her life. I was apprehensive about going to see the movie at first because I didn't want to be sitting in the movie theatre crying my eyes out because of the beatings, hangings and gross mistreatments of African Americans that I thought this movie would portray. However, when I saw the movie it took on a different perspective. Oh yes, I did cry but they were tears of joy because I witnessed a demonstration of Harriet's faith and her solid relationship with God. She was guided by the Holy Spirit and relied totally on his presence to guide her through her travels for freeing the slaves. She did not make a move without the leading of God. What Harriett had was a strong faith in what her God could do! She never wavered once but remained faithful. Faith makes things possible not easy.

I remember a time when I clearly moved in that same strong faith, like Harriet. I have two sons, Donald and Derrick and I must admit they have become some fantastic men. However, that doesn't surprise me because they were always great boys. I must admit that I was truly blessed because I never, ever had any trouble from them – no drugs, no police, and no negativity. They were always respectful, never back talking, always willing to help, super intelligent, and full of love. As my mother had introduced me to Jesus Christ as a child, I followed in her guidance and did the same. I stood on the Word of God and had faith that He would always provide and take care of them.

Donald, the oldest wanted to be an electrical engineer. He

was always a hard worker and took education seriously, maybe because of the influence of his mom, the teacher. I can remember us traveling to visit family in North Carolina and Donald studying for the SAT's in the back of the car. He had hundreds of vocabulary cards flipping them back and forth to make sure he knew their meaning. Now because of his hard work he maintained excellent grades and Drexel University partnering with Rohm and Haas gave him a $90,000 scholarship in chemical engineering. My sweet, intelligent son however, decides that he doesn't want the scholarship because he wants to be an electrical engineer. Son, are you kidding me our last name is not Rockefeller! Couldn't you have majored in chemical and minored in electrical? Jesus, take the wheel! So my son decided, with some strong coaching, that he would pursue his electrical engineering degree at Morehouse College in Atlanta, Georgia. Best choice he (we) could have ever made. "There is no obstacle too great, no challenge too difficult, if we have faith." Gordon B. Hinckley

Morehouse is a private, historically black male institution founded in 1867. Its mission is to develop men with disciplined minds who will lead lives of leadership and service, which emphasizes the intellectual and character development of its students. When we arrived twenty-five years ago, I felt this mindset throughout the entire campus. Everything was done decently and in order. Every individual that we spoke with was a positive role model for the young men whose parents were entrusting them to their care. I believed this was a great fit for my son.

The first year there was without a scholarship and we struggled with the tuition but by the grace of God we got it done. Now we are getting ready for the second year. Donald's grades continued to excel as he maintained a high grade point average. I knew we needed money for him to continue but I did not have enough. I remember going to a women's retreat and the speaker had us to put our prayer requests in a jar. The objective was that the jar would remind us that God answers our prayers. Tuition at that time was around $14,000 and since I had half of it, my request was for God to help me secure the other half for the year. When you hear how my story progressed you will see how small my thinking of God was at that time. "For we walk by faith, not by sight." 2 Corinthians 5:7 KJV

School started in August and all I knew was that my son Donald was going back to Morehouse and that God would provide. Yes, I was walking in FAITH –

"Faith shows the reality of what we hope for, it is the evidence of things we cannot see." Hebrews 11:1 NLT. So in faith, I moved like it was happening, Donald was going back to Morehouse and God took care of the rest. We needed to get to Atlanta. Larry, my brother-in-law had a travel agency and hooked us up with tickets. Faith at work! Donald needed a place to stay. His cousin Ricky was attending Clark University and had an apartment in Atlanta. Donald would just stay with him. Faith at work! Oh but it gets better. We were booked to leave for Atlanta on a Saturday morning in August. Financially, we were still at the same place, but our bags were packed and tickets were ready. I still believed, continued to walk in faith, and remained confident that my God would provide.

Friday afternoon, Donald gets a call from Morehouse stating that they saw his grade point average and wanted to know if he had a scholarship. Hold on to your seats for my God makes the impossible, possible! My son responded that he did not have a scholarship. They offered him a scholarship package that entailed tuition, room and board and was part of a 5-year master's program in conjunction with Georgia Institute of Technology, one of the leading research universities in the USA. He also had the opportunity to study abroad in London. Although this may have happened many years ago, my soul is still overwhelmed every time I think about it. My feet are still shouting all over the floor! Remember we serve a big God who wants to bless us greatly. "Little faith will bring your souls to heaven, but great faith will bring heaven to your souls." Charles Spurgeon

As I conclude, I want to challenge you with igniting your faith and keeping it alive! This is not a one-shot process, but a lifestyle. Here are some helpful strategies that have helped me through this journey. First and foremost, you want to begin with reading your Bible every day and meditating on God's Word. You will find comfort, strength, and answers to all your concerns in the Word of God. Attending a bible believing, teaching church will also help to keep your faith alive. A church with double standards, untruths, and worldly influence over Godly principles is not acceptable. God is a God of truth and excellence, not foolishness and chaos. It matters where you go to church.

The words we speak are important to igniting our faith and keeping it alive. Words have energy and power. They can encourage, heal, inspire, hold back, support, hurt, embarrass, and humble, just to name a few things. When we understand their importance, we understand the fact that we must teach and discipline ourselves to speak words of life. When Christ went to the cross, He did everything for us, like bearing our sicknesses, getting rid of our fears, and most importantly making us right with God. If we want our children saved, our finances increased, our relationships mended, and our bodies healed we must speak words of faith not destruction. Our faith must be declared every day by the words of faith that come out of our mouths. Never say that your children make you sick, but in the Name of Jesus declare that they are saved and have long, healthy lives. Never say that you are broke, but in the Name of Jesus, declare that God has a plan for your life, a plan to prosper you and give you a hope and a future (Jeremiah 29:11).

And finally, we must believe, which means walking like it's already done no matter the reality that you really don't even see it. Pack the boxes before you know where the new house is going to be located. Buy the nurses' uniform before you enter the nurse's program. Swim the yard for years before you get the pool and put up pictures so you can keep the vision in front of you. These actions are all true moves of believers who refuse to let their faith dwindle. "But without faith it is impossible to please him: for he that cometh to God must believe that he is, and that he is a rewarder of them that diligently seek him." Hebrews 11:6 KJV. I'm not blessed by the things that I have, I'm blessed by my relationship with God.

Charron Monaye

From humble beginnings to a highly sought-after writer, Charron continues to exemplify excellence while expanding her interests in marketing, coaching, film, and beyond. This award-winning author/playwright and ground-breaking writing expert have evolved into a who's who in America's Arts and Literature. As a dynamic businesswoman and writer with over twenty-five years in the industry, Charron Monaye and her pen have been a force to be reckoned with.

As Founder and Owner of Pen Legacy ®, Charron Monaye has been recognized as a Literary Game Changer who doesn't mind adapting words into legacies. She's authored 8 books (co-authored 4), published over 30 new authors, written/produced 3 theatrical productions, contributed to more than 30 book anthologies worldwide, and hired to adapt other novels into theatrical scripts such as; From Federal Prison to First Lady, Til Death Do us Part, Testify, just to name a few. In 2018, she had the opportunity to produce and premiere her sold-out stage play, "Get Out of Your Own Way" in Hollywood, California.

Utilizing many of the same tactics commonly used today, Charron Monaye gave a new meaning to what it means to "share your truth" and exemplifies just how far your truth will take you. From her then unprecedented writing techniques to the continuously innovative ways in which she uses social issues, current events, timeless messages and her expertise on scriptwriting and story-telling, Charron remains a cutting-edge writer, who pushes all boundaries.

Charron has a Bachelor of Arts in Political Science from West Chester University, Master's in Public Administration from Keller Graduate School of Management, a Certificate in Paralegal Studies and Life Coaching, and a Doctorate of Philosophy (Humane Letters) from CICA International University & Seminary. She was also appointed as "Fellow of the Most Excellent Order of International Experts (FOIE)" in the field of Entrepreneurship from the United Nations and have been awarded and recognized for her work as an Author and Playwright.

Charron is a member of Zeta Phi Beta Sorority, Inc., Order of Eastern Star and First Baptist Church of Crestmont. She resides in Wesley Chapel, FL and is a proud mother of two sons, Christopher & Craig.

Contact Info:
Business Website: www.penlegacy.com
Author Website: www.charronmonaye.com
Email: info@penlegacy.com
Facebook & Twitter: PenLegacy

Instagram: iamcharronmonaye
LinkedIn: Charron Monaye, MPA

I Refuse To Lose

If a baby boomer raised you, you were probably taught to honor the principles of work. "Work" meaning a job that you clock in for eight hours and praise God daily to have so you can pay your bills. However, what "work" actually equates to is committing hours of your life in exchange for monetary compensation, and hopefully, your job allows the opportunity to "borrow" hours to cover the time you are away from work due to an illness or a much-needed vacation. And should you have to end up caring for a family member, you must pray that you qualify for Family and Medical Leave, which is unpaid time. The system of work has been in place for centuries. Imagine being a kid, who has tons of dreams and is very ambitious, being told, "The only thing you should be focused on is graduating from high school, getting a job, and retiring. A pension is guaranteed, whereas a dream may never come true! So, stay focused."

Imagine having a gift or talent that is never allowed to manifest because you have to work and quitting your job to chase a dream is frowned upon and even considered a crazy notion by some people. Les Brown once said, "The graveyard is the richest place on earth." It took me years to understand that saying, but as I got older, I learned the graveyard is where you "find all the hopes and dreams that were never fulfilled, the books that were never written, the songs that were never sung, the inventions that were never shared, and the cures that were never discovered. All because someone was too afraid to take that first step, didn't keep with the problem, or not determined to carry out their dream." Truly understanding this message made me decide between my gift or my job, because I have yet to find a career. I thought back to when my elementary school teacher told my mother, "Charron is going to be a writer because she is so talkative." Or the time when I recited my poem "Alone" during the United Negro College Fund Banquet at the age of twelve. Or when I wrote for the Philadelphia Association of Paralegals and received reviews, press, and acknowledgements while being a staff writer.

Being a writer is who I was; it was my therapy and how I survived. Since I was never told my gift mattered just as much if not more than my income, I ignored the potential of my gift. I used it for school, writing papers for others, and correcting correspondence, but I never fully used my gift for the purpose it was intended. I used to tell myself, "If I'm not careful, I'm going to be one of those rich people in the graveyard." I would ask for help from my peers on how to hone my gift, but they would quote me some ridiculous price that I could not afford. I used Google to learn the how-tos, but without a physical person to walk with me, my dreams became extinct. Soon, I only focused on "working" to pay the bills and take care of my kids. I gave up on my gift. I couldn't afford it, and no one was willing to help me. Being a mother and employee, I could not always "borrow my time" to travel to a free event in another city so I could network or gain exposure. I knew my gift was worthy enough to be seen, but nobody knew me. So, dream voided.

But, in 2008, the recession hit. I was facing a divorce, eviction, having anxiety attacks, unemployed, and being hounded by debt collectors. I had nothing and felt like nothing. I cried so much that I had no more tears left in me to shed. My boys did everything they could to cheer me up, but it only ended up making me feel like more of a failure. Cheering me up is not something my young boys should have thought they had the responsibility to do. How could someone be doing well one day, and the next, they are so far beneath rock bottom that they would have to climb upward to reach it? I had past due bills piling up on the table and no financial help anywhere. I had shoulders to cry on, but I needed a source of income, a new life, and a savior to get back to the right side of living.

To make matters worse, I started working for a temp agency. Every day I would sit at that job highly pissed off because here I was a woman with a bachelor's degree and certification but working eight-hour days for ten-dollars an hour. My pride was shot, and if someone wanted to kill me, I would have welcomed it. You probably think I should have been grateful because at least I had a job, but it was not enough. I was barely staying afloat. However, my boys never missed a beat. I couldn't say the same for myself, missing many meals. I couldn't make them suffer for my stupidity, so I chose to suffer alone.

From that temp job, I went to work for Bell & Bell Attorney at Law as a paralegal. The pay was no better, and I went from traveling to Blue Bell to Center City, Philadelphia. Now I had the expense of gas and train fare. Things just kept getting more and more interesting, for lack of a better word. But, even with the nothingness of that job, when it came to my ego, it introduced me to entrepreneurship. During my commute on the train or while sitting at my desk at work, I would lose myself in thoughts about how great it would be to have my own business and hire others to work for me while I chill at home or escape to my beach house for the weekend. (James and Jennifer, the attorneys I worked for, did not miss a Friday at the beach.) Then I would start getting excited at the thought that my writing could make those things happen for me, but then, I could hear my dad's voice in my head saying, "You better not quit that job." My mother's voice would follow with, "You have kids to think about." Then I envisioned my boys standing there looking at me sadly, which made me quickly abort the idea. For the remainder of the train ride, I would occupy myself with reading the metro newspaper.

November 23, 2008. By then, I had lost every ounce of fight I had in me. I had to go to housing court to face the consequences of not being able to pay my rent. The apartment's attorney and the judge let me have it. Not able to afford legal representation, I had to beg for and accept assistance. Seeing my pity, the judge told the apartment's attorney to give me thirty days to come up with the back rent and court cost. *COURT COST! Just kill me, please! How the hell am I going to come up with that amount of money?* But, I humbly accepted the judgement and caught the train back to the place that was still my home.

Once home, I dropped to the floor and cried. I could barely pay the bills I had, and now there was a bill for over three thousand dollars that I had to pay before December 30, 2008. Just when I felt I had lost the fight, my oldest son Chris said, "Mommy, write about it." I hadn't written in years, and simply writing about it wouldn't get the money I needed for the payment. So, my boys and I would still end up homeless. But, instead of letting my son know I had just about given up, I forced a smile and replied, "Okay, baby. Mommy will." He wiped away my tears and sat on the floor with me. Then Craig walked over and sat in my lap. I looked at the composition book on the floor for a few moments before picking it up and starting to write.

The next day at work, I talked to James about my troubles, and he asked me if I had a gift that I could do very well. "I write," I told him, and he replied, "Then you're not broke." That day, I cried on his desk, frustrated because I didn't feel like I was capable of using my gift of writing to be successful. I was a single mom with two boys who depended on me for everything, and I had to work so that I could get a pension once I retired. I could not sacrifice anymore. James looked me, and with a strong voice, he said, "You can't let your gift die. Something in you must live for your children. Why make them suffer because of what you've been told? Some people work all their lives and don't live long enough to get their pension or social security. You must be whole and available to be their mother. You *are* very important."

Even though I'd heard what he said, what I knew about chasing dreams came to the forefront and dismissed everything he was saying. It wasn't until a producer out of Atlanta replied to one of my poems on Facebook that things started to turn around for me. I felt like my dreams were within reach. He liked my poetry and asked if I wrote songs. I replied, and he sent me three tracks to write the lyrics for. *Wait! What is going on?* I lived in Philadelphia, and he was in Atlanta. I wondered what he saw in me that people in Philly or others who I knew didn't see.

I received the tracks, had my sorority sister Summer reference them, and then sent them back. He loved them so much that he sent me more tracks and used my songs for his artists. It was amazing to hear artists singing my lyrics on commercial albums. *Is this happening?* I was finally utilizing my gift and living a dream. From that opportunity came a book deal, and I adapted that book into a stage play that I co-produced. I traveled to DC to showcase my play in the theater festival and created a publishing company through which I published other people's books as well as my own. I also formed and trademarked my business Pen Legacy® and became a coach. In 2018, premiering my play Get Out of Your Own Way in

Hollywood, California, and I accomplished all this while employed, but now with the Federal Government.

When I realized I could "work" and be an entrepreneur at the same time, the limitations that I once knew were lifted. I no longer kept my gifts in bondage, and I stopped quitting on myself because of what I was raised to believe. Even though I sometimes work harder because I am an employee and entrepreneur, the rewards and blessings come in abundance, and those things that once worried me are distant memories. I will never forget the year 2008 because it made me realize I need my gift to survive. I need the blessings that it brings to thrive. I need the therapy that writing provides, which lets me live with anxiety without any issues. This gift has many purposes, and now that I am utilizing it, life for me has gotten so much better. God is smiling down on me. The "right" people know me, many people want to learn from me, and others enjoy working with me. My bills are paid, my credit is great, and my kids are flourishing. Most importantly, my boys and I are rich on earth and living in our wealth. It gets no better than that.

If you are living life with untapped dreams or goals, use my story as motivation. Sometimes I wonder what my life would be like now if I hadn't waited so long to use my gifts blessed upon me. I remember being in Schmidt Hall on West Chester University campus, and my boyfriend Hasan used to tell me, "You are such a great writer." Even back then, I used to smile at his compliment but ignore him at the same time. I never imagined my writing could bring me to the place where I am now or make what was once impossible possible. I had many people who did believe in me, but when certain ideals, principles, and rules are instilled in a person, it is hard for them to see the options available to them during their journey. So, remember this. Even if you are working a job, you can still manifest your dreams. I know tons of people who are still working a nine-to-five but living out their dream by utilizing their gifts or passions. With the pressures of the day-to-day hustle of life, wouldn't it feel good to be able to do something you enjoy and possibly get paid for it? Wouldn't you feel that much inspired or worthy of life if you were living to enjoy it instead of only living to work and eventually die?

The graveyard is the richest place on earth, but it doesn't have to be. Use my testimony to motivate you, and if you need my coaching services to help you tap in so you can enjoy your gifts on this side of Earth, then I can help you with that. Trust me, doing so will be far more rewarding, fulfilling, and legendary for you and your family than you sitting on your dreams. For me, the greatest reward received after tapping into my gift is the fact that my children now have a business that they can collect on, work for, and operate for the rest of their lives. Even after I depart from this earth, they will continue to receive royalties from everything my name is on that is sold or purchased. My businesses are now inheritances that will carry them and the next generations to come. Being a single mother, for me to know I will be able to leave them with a successful business rather than draining debt is a good feeling. So, even though my mind was taught to work for a pension, being an entrepreneur has given me the opportunity to create something that will outlive me here on earth and continue to sustain others even when I am in the graveyard.

The Legacy Continues

Congratulations to the Pen Legacy Family
for hitting Amazon Best Selling List…

PenLegacy

BRUISED BROKEN & BLESSED

CONFIDENCE Unlocked
KIAWANA KEY

STOP Asking For Permission & Give Notice !!
CHARRON MONAYE

How I Survived Without Chemo Therapy
SABRINA KOShR

GET OUT OF YOUR OWN WAY
Charron Monaye

Love THE REAL YOU
CHARRON MONAYE

Passing As Straight

BAD BITCHES AND POWER PITCHES
For Women Entrepreneurs and Speakers Only

from CAREFREE to CAREGIVER
A 31 DAY DEVOTIONAL
TERALEEN R. CAMPBELL

Congratulations to
our Amazon Bestsellers

WE ARE
#1

CHARRON MONAYE'S
Book Anthology Collection
5 BOOKS, 55 INSPIRATIONAL STORIES
Pen Legacy Presents
Get Out of Your Own Way
Overcoming Adversity to Live In Your Truth Out Loud
Compiled by
Charron Monaye
GET OUT OF YOUR OWN WAY
11 Life-Changing Stories on How To Enjoy the Journey & Stay Focused
Compiled by
Charron Monaye
BRUISED BROKEN & BLESSED
Life Changing Stories That Will Ignite Hope, Elevate Personal Growth and Confirm Your Greatness
Foreword by Brittany Garth
Compiled by Charron Monaye & Shontaye Hawkins, MBA
SLAY YOUR LEGACY
9 KEYS TO MANIFESTING THE LIFE YOU WANT
LIMITED EDITION
Compiled by Charron Monaye
Foreword by Andrel Harris
Get Out of Your Own Way
11 GAME-CHANGING STORIES ON MASTERING THE POWER OF TRUST, FAITH & SUCCESS
CHARRON MONAYE
"When Your Pen Becomes Your Legacy"
WWW.PENLEGACY.COM

Pen Legacy

SHINE BRIGHT ON
42ND STREET IN NEW YORK
Visit www.penlegacy.com to get yours today.

Pen Legacy Publishing

Check out our catalog.

Journals/Guides

Boss Moves Start With You: 2018 Self-Reflection Journal & Vision Planner by: Briana McKnight

Maximizing Your Tax Refund Made Easy! by: Khristina Barnes

2018 Legacy Journal & Planner: A Planning Tool for your Freedom & Future by: Charron Monaye

I Matter Journal by: Charron Monaye

Secure Your Legacy Journal by: Charron Monaye

Book Anthologies

Bruised, Broken, and Blessed: Life Changing Stories That Will Ignite Hope, Elevate Personal Growth, and Confirm Your Greatness compiled by Charron Monaye & Shontaye Hawkins

Get Out Of Your Own Way: Overcoming Adversity to Live In Your Truth Out Loud compiled by: Charron Monaye

Get Out Of Your Own Way: 11 Life-Changing Stories on How to Face Everything & Rise! by Charron Monaye

Get Out of Your Own Way: 11 Game-Changing Stories on Mastering the Power of Trust, Faith & Success by: Charron Monaye

Divine Connections: Experiencing the Joy of God's Divine Order by: Barbara Allen

Slay Your Legacy: 9 Keys to Manifesting The Life You Want by: Charron Monaye
Put A Nail End IT: Purpose Begins At The End Of Your Comfort Zone by: Kiawana Leaf

LGBT
Passing As Straight: Beautiful Women Whose True Sexuality Went Undetected by a Judgmental Society by: Kinyatta Gray
From Section 8 To C.E.O by: Kinyatta Gray

Devotional
Embracing Your New Normal: A 21 Day Devotional to Encourage & Support You As You Move On by: Teraleen Campbell

Inspirational/Personal Development
Respect Your Choices: Finding Balance in Success By: Vaughn McNeill
STOP Asking for Permission & Give Notice: How To Accept & Attain Who You Are Without Validation by: Charron Monaye
Let Me Tell You Like I Told Myself: Love's Truth Never Changes by: Summer Willow Fitch
The Power of Shut Up by: Lisa Dove Washington
STOP Asking for Permission & Give Notice: How To Accept & Attain Who You Are Without Validation by: Charron Monaye
Don't Give Up Too Soon: 10 Ways to Help You ReSET your Energy, Wellness, & Tranquility by: Tinesha Boswell
Confidence Unlocked by: Kiawana Key
Beautiful Toxicity by: Ontaria Kim Wilson

3,655 Miles To Kismet by: Parenthysis E. Gardner

Fear Is A Crime: How To Overcome Fear & Face Your Destiny by Charron Monaye

STOP Asking for Permission & Give Notice: How To Accept & Attain Who You Are Without Validation by: Charron Monaye

Beautifying Sins: I am guilty of my sins but that's what makes me beautiful, because I have been cleansed! By: Kiawana Leaf

Overcoming by: Andrel Harris

Children's Book

John's Journey to Outer Space by: John Xavier

Business/Entrepreneur

I Want To Quit My Job: 8 Entrepreneurial Strategies for Massive Results While Employed by Charron Monaye

Sanctify Your Money: The 11th Commandment by: Toni Moore

Bad Bitches and Power Pitches: For Women Entrepreneurs and Speakers Only by: Precious Williams

90 Days of Forever: Unlock Your Financial Future and Change Your Life by: Nicole Deas

Christian Fiction

MisLeading Lady by: Sharon Y. Judie

Poetry

UnBreak My Heart: From Scorn to Finding Love Again by: Charron Monaye

My Side of the Story: From a Woman Waiting to Exhale by:
Charron Monaye

Parenting/Caregiver
From CAREFREE to CAREGIVER: A 31 Devotional to
Balance, Encourage, and Support You in Your New Role by:
Teraleen Campbell
Shattering the Barriers of Single Motherhood: A Single
Mom's guide to Power, Resilience, and the Pursuit of
Happiness by: Sang Thi Duong

Fiction
Leonard Smith by: AJ Harrison

Memoirs
The Black Blood In My Heart by: La'Mena Marie
How I Survived Without Chemotherapy: One Woman's
Story From Diagnosed To Thriving by: Sabrina Moore
Stop Being a Doormat & Start Being a Boss by: Toni Moore
The Woodshed by: Jaguar Wright
From the Basement to the Stage by: Darnell Richardson Jr.

30 Days: Surviving the Trauma and Unexpected Loss of a
Single Parent as an Only Child by: Kinyatta Gray

Share This Book!

Retail Price $24.99

Special Quantity Discounts

5-20 Books	$17.95 each
21-99 Books	$15.95 each
100-499 Books	$12.95 each
500-999 Books	$9.95 each
1000+ Books	$6.95 each

To Place An Order Contact: info@penlegacy.com

www.ingramcontent.com/pod-product-compliance
Lightning Source LLC
Chambersburg PA
CBHW051121300726

48981CB00021B/496/J